T0131619

What's Next?

Exploring the Journey of Souls in the Afterlife

Written and Illustrated by

A S T R I D   S T R O M B E R G

BALBOA
PRESS

A DIVISION OF HAY HOUSE

Balboa Press books may be ordered through booksellers or by contacting:

Balboa Press
A Division of Hay House
1663 Liberty Drive
Bloomington, IN 47403
www.balboapress.com
1 (877) 407-4847

Because of the dynamic nature of the Internet, any web addresses or
links contained in this book may have changed since publication and
may no longer be valid. The views expressed in this work are solely those
of the author and do not necessarily reflect the views of the publisher,
and the publisher hereby disclaims any responsibility for them.

The author of this book does not dispense medical advice or prescribe the use
of any technique as a form of treatment for physical, emotional, or medical
problems without the advice of a physician, either directly or indirectly. The
intent of the author is only to offer information of a general nature to help you
in your quest for emotional and spiritual well-being. In the event you use any
of the information in this book for yourself, which is your constitutional right,
the author and the publisher assume no responsibility for your actions.

Front cover photo taken by Kim Porth.
Author's portrait taken by Beatrice A Ruini, photographer

Print information available on the last page.

ISBN: 978-1-5043-3245-3 (sc)
ISBN: 978-1-5043-3246-0 (hc)
ISBN: 978-1-5043-3247-7 (e)

Library of Congress Control Number: 2015907234

Balboa Press rev. date: 05/18/2015

Contents

Part 1

The Journey

Part 2

Questions and Answers from Spirit

Part 3
Prayers and Exercises

Acknowledgments

From my heart and soul, I acknowledge and thank first and foremost my amazing husband, Eric. I love you in more dimensions than one. Love you, darling!

Zoltan and Kyali, my children, I am so blessed to have you in my life. You mean the world to me! Keep the book for when you feel inspired to read it. Some parts are even funny!

Teri, thank you for initiating, supporting, and working through this book with me. You are a dear friend indeed.

I also want to thank my family and those who have crossed my life with meaning in the past. There are too many souls to mention. I look back at you, at our shared experiences, and at who I was back then, and I love you for helping me grow in such a way that I became who I am today.

I thank the wonderful team at BalboaPress and my dear PR friends, Bruce and Leonna Merrin for believing in the book, its message, and where it comes from. Your support has been invaluable.

Last but not least I thank the spirits and the souls who have come through to deliver this book of hope and empowerment to those who read it. Our search for ourselves is never-ending, and although we may have tough times with it, the wonderland you present to our unseeing eyes holds the magic of love we share with those in the afterlife and beyond.

Introduction

When I was 20, I had a dream. My dad was in a castle tower where he was imprisoned. He found his way out through a tiny window and walked away in the distance via the castle walls. Three months later, my dad died. He later appeared to his mother at the tomb telling her he was fine and that he loved her. He came to me a few months later with the same message. This wouldn't be the first, nor the last time a deceased soul came to visit and talk to me.

Since birth, I have been hearing, feeling, smelling and seeing spirits and souls departed. They were my friends as a child, they were my angel guardians growing up, they are now the many souls and entities I connect with on a daily basis. They have helped me grow, become a better person and enlightened me as to who we are and why we do what we do. To me, they, we, all come from what I call Brilliant Essence, the essence of our brilliant beings. I have a passion for Brilliant Essence. I see it in everyone and everything: soul connection, soul seeing. Brilliant Essence is what you may call source or divine consciousness that flows through all. It is the universal intelligence that guides us to be, to live, to evolve and expand in everything that is, has been or may be. It is through Brilliant Essence that I see the potential, the issues and the solutions of those I meet. Brilliant Essence speaks to me through the voices of souls past, and this book reflects what it says about their journey in the afterlife. Where are you going? Where have you gone? Are you ok? We cry out to those who leave us. Our experience of death is one of separation, and yet we are never really truly separated.

This book came about after a question was asked to me triggering a flow of responses on the afterlife my friend Teri suggested I write. Throughout my life, souls departed have shared with me so many dimensions and worlds they experienced, but sharing it was extravagant, controversial, and sometimes impolite. As many of our kind were told, I was too sensitive, overly emotional, and very imaginative. I took it upon myself to break the barrier of judgment and write this book to help those who cannot talk to the departed like I do so they may find solace, strength and hope in what lies ahead after death.

This book gives you insight into the worlds that we connect to and transition in and out of. Death is change, and change entails transition. In the first part of this book, souls describe the journey from death to rebirth. What happens when you die? Where do you go? What do you do? In part 2, souls answer questions: Do you meet God? What about religion? I channel specific souls from beyond to give you a perspective of their experiences. As you will see, as skeptical as I may be myself toward these connections, the messages delivered are inspiring and fun. Lastly, in part 3, I offer you prayers and exercises. I was born and raised Catholic. I was always critical of the sermons and interpretations and read the Bible several times when I was young, liking the apostles in particular. I go sporadically to church these days. God speaks to me fine here, at home, in more ways than one! I pray many times a day and appreciate my religious background for its power to have served me so well, especially growing in love, understanding, and wonder. Being crazy to believe fairies exist, that divine consciousness exists, that after death there is a plethora of life to choose from—to me, it's just part of the picture of expanding evolution of thought through our lives as souls.

Whatever your beliefs, I hope you take this account as an idea of the many options to choose from in life and in death. With, in and through loving light on what may be, we become to better be. Enjoy the read!

PART 1

The Journey

Where souls go, glory follows.

At the Time of Death

At the time of death, the body is left behind. Little by little, the soul lets go of its earthly attachments. The physical attachments leave first. As it departs, it does not feel the touch of the hand on its dead body. The nerves no longer compute with its state of being. The jaw does not open when the soul seeks to speak. The legs do not respond when the soul desires to rise. Yet the soul still perceives and is conscious of itself and its surroundings. Without ears, it hears everything. Without touch, it feels everything. Without sight, it sees everything. The soul's senses are still alive, and a sense of self remains. The soul still has identity. To best understand how a soul can still be a soul without a body, imagine that the soul is like a Russian doll, one inside of another, inside of another, and so on. The smallest of these dolls may be the soul in a body. Once the body gone, the soul is a bigger doll. The biggest of them all would be the ultimate soul that encompasses all that is. You might call that soul God.

At the time of death, the soul detaches from physicality and is drawn to its greatest self that encompasses more of a person's self than we can ever imagine. During the time of transition from death to the afterlife, the soul realizes it is dead to our world in body. It realizes its loss of earthly connections and sensations. It also realizes it can go places just by thought. However, all physical chemistry is over, done, let go of. Our bodies are mostly made of chemical energy, and once that chemistry is over, the chemical connections disappear. Taste and smell leave first. There is no mouth or palate with which to taste, no olfactory senses to smell the roses. Sexuality is dead too; the hormonal urge is gone. There is no brain to attach thought to physical pleasures, but thought still exists.

Just as in life, there are souls who move quickly through death and those who take their time. For some, the process is fast. Within days, they've revisited everyone they loved, whispered their good-byes, and moved on to heaven. They do not have much to deal with, as they have followed their soul guidance well, paid their dues before leaving, and can rest in peace while helping others from yonder. Others have a tougher time. They may have jolted themselves out of life. If they leave via an accident, a murder, or a suicide, these souls need time to regain a sense of their identity, an understanding of who they are and sometimes even the will to move on. To mediums—people who connect with the departed—these souls sometimes feel stuck. They may be "heavy" to be around and often portray their worst attitudes because that's exactly what's holding them back. Some may even bring havoc to households of people who don't know what to do but to blame the person beside them. If only they knew it may be a poor soul asking for help to transition!

Every soul's journey is unique, but they may share some similarities; they leave the earthly plane and find themselves out of body, they say their goodbyes, they heal themselves of what may have burdened them through life, they revisit their past thoughts and actions and they choose, or not, to reincarnate.

Three Days to Say Good-bye

One of the commonalities reported by souls in the afterlife is a three day period that follows the time of death during which the departing soul says goodbye to its loved ones. During those three days the vibrational earthly connections of the departed soul are still relatively strong and the soul can fairly easily connect with its loved ones to appear or express its farewell. Saying farewell is never easy for us. It's sometimes a heart-wrenching tug of war. It's not something we ever do well. Saying goodbye is not natural to the soul. In the afterlife, farewells do not exist because the soul recognizes its universality and considers itself one with all, always. Farewells exist only in this type of life, where we have a limited understanding of ourselves and we believe ourselves to be separate entities that may never see each other again. What farewells do is signal the end of an experience and the beginning of a new way to be together, this time, without the body being involved.

Departing souls still have a sense of self, but the bodies are gone. So what else is there? The departing ones become fast aware that a new journey has begun.

They basically birth themselves into another state of being. Once they had bodies; now they are without. This is huge for the soul. It has to accept the fact that it just is, as it is, for now. Self-realization always comes first. It's like waking up in the morning and saying, "Oh, this is who I am! Yeah, I remember!" Then comes the situation. Where am I? What am I doing here? What's happening? What do I relate to? The departed soul finds itself in a new situation where being has a new time and place. Some have zapped out fast, met their departed loved ones, taken account of their new surroundings, and come back strongly to say good-bye to everyone. They understand their new state of consciousness fast, maneuver through it with remembrance of past deaths experienced, and have a strong sense of connection to their loved ones left behind, and the passing is fast. Others refuse to acknowledge their new state and pass to the other side with difficulty. They see their dead bodies and don't know what to do or where to go. They don't see any light, and they haven't a clue how to reconnect with their loved ones to say good-bye. These souls stay in limbo until something changes. Saying good-bye does not come easily to some and may not happen for a long time.

For those transitioning easily, also comprised in the three days after death is the life review. This is what some call being at the gates of heaven and asking permission to go in. What does a soul have to say for itself at the gates of heaven? Life as it was previously experienced floods back with every sense expressed in the moment, spoken or not. Words, actions, and thoughts are reviewed. If you said or thought something to uplift someone, you will see the power of your word as you drive through to the afterlife. If you said or thought bad things, you will face them again, and their repercussions. The soul transitions with the realization of the alignments it has left behind and those it continues to hold within its experience beyond. This is why it is not recommended to commit suicide. Giving up one's life is acknowledged in the afterlife and perpetuates through one's connections into the livelihoods of others still living, affecting them in really sad ways. Your soul holds itself responsible in the afterlife—as it should in this one!

Saying goodbye is really important for those left behind. This is the time when they have a chance to let go of the connections that hold the departing soul back. Everything negative is to be let go of, and the light and love of the spirit are to be celebrated. We have three days to remind the departing soul of our love. These three days are the strongest days of connection they have with us in the material realm. Have you ever been woken up in the early morning with a deceased loved one shouting your name in your ear? Has your child ever seen the ghost of a departed grandma in the house on the night of her departure? During the three days after the moment of death, physical connections to the soul are still strong, and the departing soul, through will and desire, can appear in physical ways to those of us left behind. After that, the enlightened soul transitions into the light. The darker souls may close the door to the light and dwell in darkness.

The Passing

Those who have had near-death experiences have reported passages into the afterlife. They may flat-line, be in a coma, or be placed in the fridge with a tag, and then their bodies "start up" again out of nowhere—and they remember their experience! Many report similar experiences of the passing. The common denominator for children passing is the experience of crossing a bridge, going through a tube of light, or over a rainbow. Adults take a boat, go through a tunnel, or find themselves on a shore. Those who have bad experiences report either being nowhere or in some kind of hell, sometimes even with flames or monsters, or feeling very much alone. Those who have a good experience may see their deceased loved ones, angels, religious figures, and even God personified.

People who have near-death experiences are always told or signaled to come back to life, whether by choice or duty. Souls who don't come back find that their time, whether chosen or not, is up, and they move on. Some don't completely leave this world. Some don't know how. They haven't let go, and they stick around in their own parallel reality. There is no passage per se. There is only another reality. When a soul is lost, it will call out to its dear ones or anyone capable of aligning and communicating with it. People who are in tune will immediately understand and see, hear or feel these lost souls. The call could be just a thought in your mind, the appearance of a dark entity in the house, or abnormal manifestations of emotions around you such as anger and frustration let loose and expressed through nearby animals or kids. These are signals that there may be a lost soul on the loose to be taken care of. The darker the soul's expression is in the afterlife, the darker its place of contact to you, alive here on Earth. Watch out for negativity!

Helping to pass a soul demands strength in love and light. If you feel a lost soul around you, the fastest way for a win-win situation is to send out the most loving and uplifting thought. You might want to hand the task to superiors of love and light, such as archangels or mentors you trust, to help the soul transition. If, on the other hand, you sense positivity and love, return the thought immediately! The more love, the lighter and faster the passing for the departing soul. Souls transitioning always have a light coming their way. For some, light engulfs them instantly and completely. They mention being engulfed into the light and feeling utter and complete bliss. Unconditional love overtakes them and soon thereafter, they find themselves in heaven; a place so filled with love that no negativity could penetrate. There, although individuality may persist, negative emotions and personal traits are gone. There is only love, understanding and well-being. For others, the light comes as a beacon. This is the divine sign that heaven awaits. Within the light may come forth one or several deceased loved ones to accompany the transitioning soul into the light. However, not all souls take heed of this light and they may wander, their backs to it, never quite lifting off to reunite with their greater soul loving self.

Souls report many different experiences in the timing of their passing. For some it all happens like a flash—one minute alive, the next minute in the midst of divine bliss where there is no time. Others find themselves for quite some time between heaven and the earthly experience they left behind. They do not experience the blissful state, but rather, a state of relative well-being where personalities are maintained, and where the idea of form, emotion, negativity and time exist. Some souls report having gone straight to hell while others report wavering between realities, or going from one to another, depending on their state of consciousness and their desire to access better states of being.

It seems that the passing is one that is mostly controlled by the will of the greater soul of a person rather than the preconceived notions of life and death when alive. As the soul lets go of its physical reality, it is the power of the love toward itself that drives it to the next place to be in the afterlife. Lacking this self-love, the soul may not go to heaven where it regains understanding of its greater self. Instead, it will continue to live out its expectations of self in a smaller minded way until it is able to reunite with its greater self in love and light.

Judgment Day

It may take seconds or eons for this day to happen, but every soul, alive or dead, goes through the process of self-judgment. I remember, as a teen, warning friends about committing suicide and having to return to life later to pay their dues. A few years later, spirit (soul consciousness) was warning me that time had collapsed and karma had become an instant bitch. Today this is truer than ever. In fact, what you place your attentions on now will appear almost instantly in your life, one way or another. Judgment day takes care of reviewing our connections and what we made of them in mind, body, and spirit. Religions talk about an ultimate judgment day at the end times, when God separates the good doers from the bad, casting the bad ones in an eternal hell and allowing the good doers through the gates of heaven to infinite bliss. I believe God to be of the highest love, evolving through us all, so perhaps since then God has had a change of mind and heart as to the infinity of hell we may go to. After all, forgiveness, repentance, and trial and error have allowed a soul to redemption and salvation, and their day of judgment has ended.

Judgment day may happen in a flash after death, or may be dealt with in realms where time exists in the company of others. During the process of self-judgment or life review, other souls are there to help and the life review may take many forms. Some souls report their review as similar to watching a film about themselves and the people they engaged with in life. They see how past actions affected the lives of those they touched and vice versa—how they were affected by the actions of others. Other souls report having group sessions with fellow souls on the other side. These small gatherings are pleasant and even funny as souls joke about their past personalities and the attitudes they had. Far from being judged by their peers, souls participating in these gatherings help each other in letting go of any past self-judgment they may still have, especially around personality traits their old bodies hung onto, such as bad habits they may have been ashamed of at the time, or actions they want to redeem themselves of.

Souls who have done harm to others or themselves go on separate paths. Those who have hurt themselves or committed suicide spend time healing first, after which they may choose to work to help incoming hurt souls as repentance. From the standpoint of those left behind in life, these souls are hard to reach for many weeks, months, and sometimes even years. Faith invites the living to pray daily for them as we are told they may not have the strength to uplift themselves from beyond without them.

The space of judgment is more a state of being than an actual place. However, considering souls connect via alignments they hold, such a space does in fact exist in many ways, characterized by the desire of those souls to purify themselves further to be able to go to more blissful states of being such as heaven. In certain such spaces, lost souls connect and their space of action is as vast as the many dimensions they come from. For the bad guys who hurt and killed without heart, their life review is matched to the initial blueprint they originally came in with. Should their actions be in sync with what they came in to do, including the pain and suffering they engaged in, they return to those alignments in the afterlife to live the full circle of their karmic debt. Once an abuser, now abused, these souls will return fast to a new life where they will experience the opposite, oftentimes in the hardest environments where pain is the standard and life is all about growing into a better person through it. Others land in hell, where the pain and suffering they dealt out in life is handed back to them to experience in death, with little way out. As if the universal mind had decided to burn these soul alignments to never come back, hell is where the gunk of our humanity lies, in its own space, where few would ever venture lest they be held in temptation.

Judgment day also reflects to the soul the difference between which state it came in with before birth and which one it leaves with at the time of death. Anything less than what it came in with will be judged. Consequences of self-judgment can lead a soul to specific places of bliss, healing, repentance or self-condemnation. One of these places is indeed hell.

Hell Exists

There are too many testimonies to tell, but hell does exist. For some, Earth is their closest stop into hell. For others, it's a pit stop worth turning around in. Alignments of pain, torture, horror, and extreme fear exist. Just like with the good, the bad can also be created, and if you don't think we have enough proof of that on Earth, then sayonara! I for one do not wish to experience more.

The floor of my bedroom opened up at least twice when I was a child. Below, I saw fire, screams, and faces twisted in sheer pain. Utter horror for a five year old. The only saving grace was the presence of Mother Mary, who was showing me this by my bed. I prayed. I poured out my heart in empathy and asked Mother Mary why. Hell is where an aspect of self resides, she said. Souls do exist in hell. There souls experience emotions tangled and stuck in patterns of belief, reliving and reproducing the same constant pain, anger, fear, and worst of all, the loss of will to better states of being.

In hell, the soul relives its worst over and over again, alone or in the company of others. Nobody seems capable of helping anyone else other than to further the connections they already bear. Love is not apparent. Self-love seems absent. Everyone complains, cries, suffers, and does nothing about it. Some souls scream out for us to believe in God while they themselves still have trouble doing it for their own salvation. Hell is the ultimate never-ending nightmare.

Hell has levels of existence. Hell partly exists on Earth through the alignments to pain and suffering experienced here. Some souls are more remote to the infinite fires of hell, while others are plunged in and can't seem to get out. A soul that cannot get out is stuck in the belief there is no way out and is locked in vibrational alignments to hellish situations. However, even in hell, light can penetrate and lift up the spirits to a better place. It takes the strength of one in the highest heavens to fish out a soul in hell. Even then, the soul may not want to leave. Some souls stuck in such hellish places simply believe this is the next stage of their journey and may even think they will wake up one day and it will all be gone. The problem is their point of focus is so intently connected to the space, it would take a big change of heart and mind to make a difference, and when souls are in hell, they usually don't have too much heart or mind left to help themselves.

In parts of hell you see people wandering around like zombies. They don't care; they don't think. They have no sense of who they are or their purpose. If a soul has not been able to, or wanted to go to the light of the afterlife, they will be wanderers in dark places where their lack of bliss matches those of others. Hell does not tempt more than heaven does. We live an alignment to hell when we live the pain and suffering we inflict upon others and ourselves. Souls beyond encourage us to always do our best to connect consciously and willingly to better alignments and to love, love, love ourselves and others!

Healing Centers

Every hurt soul that passes into the light goes through a healing process. This is necessary for the soul's identity to regroup before it can proceed to higher venues. To move on, the soul needs to recognize who it is and where it is.

Healers help with this. Healers welcome the passing hurt soul and invite it to the healing center. This can look like anything from a tent set up in a desert to a sci-fi space center with the latest techniques available. Imagination helps transformation and souls know this, but as with life, alignments in death are key, and where the soul goes will depend on what it is most familiar with in the state of being it is in as the evolved soul in the afterlife.

When a hurt soul comes in, it may come accompanied or be on its own, drawn to healing by its own free will. Some souls are so hurt and confused they are literally lifted up by their angel guardians. The power of the passing can drive through the furthest call for help, and help is always present. Healing centers are available to everyone at any given time, including lost souls.

Souls looking for healing may come in droves at a time, like at a time of war on Earth. They may appear as if just coming from their worst nightmare. Still so strongly aligned with what just happened, confused, in the belief of pain without feeling it and thanks to the drive of their faith, they appear, sometimes accompanied en masse, toward the healing centers. Healing centers are like hospitals, where souls come in with different problems to be treated. Each soul is then assigned a place to stay, alone or with others, while healing begins.

The healing process can be as fast as going through a channel of light as the soul passes in a flash from death to light, or it can involve a sense of time, like going to a clinic, being taken care of, letting go of the unwanted, and finally being able to step further into the light. Some souls instantly pass through the beam of light, and the next thing they know, they are in heaven, bliss having lifted them up and away to paradise, and anything negative having simply dropped off as dust. Once healed, the soul retrieves itself to where it needs to be for its next experience of self.

Lift off to Other Realms

Interestingly, departed loved ones do not appear to communicate from the same spaces in the afterlife. When asked about this, souls explain that it is a question of vibrational alignment and their different realms and realities. When souls lift off into the light, they move on according to their evolved soul consciousness into different worlds and dimensions.

Some souls have been going back and forth between life and the afterlife for eons. With this experience, their return to the afterlife strengthens their ability to move to higher levels of self-experience, including that of merging completely with the light. In other words, souls are capable of becoming one through what I call our Brilliant Essence, their ultimate essence, and can completely let go of all ego to merge as one with all that is. On Earth, many masters have been able to completely evaporate even their physical bodies to merge with the elements of life, disappearing and reappearing at will. Souls departed may do so by aligning to their Brilliant Essence. Enlightened souls seek to merge with their ultimate essence in light. They are not soul-less. They are soul-filled! These are the souls whose ego has grown in selfless identification for their greatest self-realization as one. The ultimate experience for them is that of singularity.

Afterlife realms are very much like different continents under one umbrella, or infinite dimensions layered one over another, each dimension holding spaces where the soul may live in, like vibration of consciousness. The higher you go, the more in unity you are, and the greater you become as a soul consciousness of many. Ultimately, the soul who has reached the greatest consciousness of all is the one who has explored every part of its great self, engaging in every aspect of it all. This is the soul I call God.

God is in us all. Like a big sun with its many rays of alignments explored of itself, souls bring forth God-consciousness in its experience of itself in all realms. A soul consciousness may still desire to experience individualism before merging as one. To this end, identity and differences are key to the existence of the soul and its experience of self.

In some realms, we meet heavenly souls who are so light and bright they hold no form. They don't need it. They explore their consciousness as a breeze, a thinking wave that can permeate matter. These souls are exceptionally powerful, I find, as they can transcend their state at will, incorporate matter here on Earth, such as a cloud, or the leaves of a tree, and appear to the naked eye. Have you seen faces in the skies before? Has your child ever recognized shapes of animals and birds in rocks and mountains? These are the consciousness of souls of beings past that in the afterlife decide to come without form, through form. In other realms we find souls who keep their past looks vibrant and identifiable. Their soul consciousness still desires embodiment. It also helps them continue to connect and communicate with us here on Earth, helping us recognize them from our limited state of consciousness. However, just to throw you a curve ball, I once spoke to my deceased dad, who showed me how, as much as I was here, I was there too. We are much more than a soul, as we know it. We are soul consciousness.

To go from one realm to another needs connectivity. Some souls in the afterlife will not reconnect with some of the souls they met in their previous life. They have both lost connection to each other's vibrational level and are in their own realms of existence. Other souls will live an existence with their loved ones they reunite with. Some souls may go between realms, such as those who have attachments in one and yet prefer to resonate in another. Parents from a previous life may come to their children past. Pets may appear and disappear. I know my grandmother and my dad, for instance, are not always in the same space in the afterlife. My dad seems to be more of a helper with light-workers beyond, whereas my grandmother seems to be more attuned with the angelic realms.

In their description of their afterlife realm, I have found that deceased loved ones will come through with recognizable features and a world looking similarly like ours, except nicer! Nature has auras of color we do not have here, yet corridors and doors exist just like in our homes or offices. Animals roam freely, people mingle with glee. The afterlife has its paradise!

The Temple of Knowledge

I remember visiting the Temple of Knowledge during a past-life regression I did for myself. I found myself standing at the foot of an impressive set of curving stone stairs that wrapped around the building as well as led to the main entrance. People walked all around me as I stared at the massive dome in front of me. It felt very familiar. I knew I had been in there many times, as you would your local library. When spirits tell of this place, it is always with respect for what it stands for. The Temple of Knowledge is a landmark in the afterlife realms.

I sometimes wondered if the Temple of Knowledge wasn't another wishful idea that seemed obvious to imagine in any world of wonder. It was only years later when my five-year-old son described the buildings he knew about in the afterlife that I got validation. The Temple of Knowledge is all made of crystals, he said. There they learn. All these buildings connect. I had never told him about this before, and his descriptions match the many similar ones spirit shares with me: a massive building with a towering, dome-like top made of crystals, with huge stairs of stone or marble running up to it. It seems natural that the temple would be made of crystals. Crystals have the ability to retain information. Stories abound about how crystals hold data related to humanity and life on Earth. Crystals are able to upload and download this information, and we are able to tap into and retrieve it.

Once inside the Temple of Knowledge, it's as if the walls move. Your intention guides you to where you may find the answer, and if in doubt, the soul will always be greeted by a helper who looks like a librarian and will tell you exactly where to go. If you are looking for the Akashic records, the place where life records are held, you will go there. If you want to visit the wall of threads where threads of life are displayed, you will go there. If you want to meet up with students in a room of communication, you will go there. But you also may roam through the halls, go up and down stairs, find yourself peeking into grand study rooms, or hear the laughter and voices in classrooms you pass. Books galore, fancy computer-like virtual screens, huge globes that souls look into to see life in other worlds are all in the Temple of Knowledge.

In the Temple of Knowledge classrooms abound. They are so much fun! From the youngest to the oldest, souls participate in group exercises to help them with their growth and future lives. I remember being a tiny baby soul in a big bubble with about fifteen other baby souls in bubbles in the same class. We were all laughing so hard, bumping each other around the room, floating in our bubbles, trying to direct it to go here or there. It was our training to move with thought. Like crazy space bumper cars, we would crash, flip, and roll around, and we laughed and laughed and laughed.

Spirits have always shown me a good time in classrooms. It's all about developing skills and abilities to move forward. Souls choose their classes or are encouraged to take them by their guides. They are not always easy, and classes can include preparation for the worst in life. To an outsider, this can shock. Shame, guilt, and imprisonment may all be part of the class. The soul prepares to recognize circumstances extremely different from where they currently are, and to identify situations on the blueprint (their life map) before experiencing them helps the reborn soul remember its purpose. Doing this within a group of souls about to or having already experienced the same thing helps the soul too. Those who have already gone through are able to expound on potentials and pitfalls. For newbies, it's a time to prepare for what is to come.

Study rooms are different from classrooms in that there is no group to work with, but a master or a guide may be there to help. These rooms are used for research, testing, and practicing and are kept silent. Discreet telepathic communication only! They say anything related to having earthly emotions is done in labs because they can be contained and not shared. There is no shortage of study groups, just like there is no shortage of space anywhere in the Temple of Knowledge. Nobody stays in line waiting for a turn. The moment they transfer themselves within those walls, space and knowledge come instantly.

In study rooms you will find many preparing their future blueprints. Destiny, fate, action/reaction, gravity, cycles, rhythms of the heart and mind ... the soul who enters a body needs to be aligned. It must be able to sustain itself and grow. From the minutest cells in the body to everything else, a soul that comes to Earth is well prepared. Luckily, the soul has grown and remembers through its experiences, so from the stone to the star, the soul always comes back in individual form with what it already has, as its backbone or threads within the blueprint. Does that mean that to be a rock-star you need to have been a musician? No! That's the great part of it all. You get to do what you want. The soul can be and do what it wants. It knows, however, how much alignments count in the matter. Therefore, for those coming back to life, study rooms are places of exploration as well as spaces where decisions are made. One of the bigger study-room areas I have visited involves learning about communication between souls departed and souls left behind. Souls interested in communicating with their loved ones on Earth may learn and practice to do so. Some souls with specific gifts in that arena are involved in helping them communicate. In certain labs, some souls on Earth track down those who are open to such communication.

Labs are also vast and are separated according to tasks. Social labs, chemical labs, dictation labs—they go on and on. In the afterlife, souls still strive to evolve in any way they can. What is it like to live on Earth in a billion years? The labs can tell you the potential worlds of the future. How to better communicate with other vibrational intelligence? Labs explore. Action and reaction, mechanisms and patterns, trial and error, or empowerment of co-creation—all these things and more hold the space for souls departed to continue to grow. The temple of knowledge is a powerhouse of information for all souls in the afterlife.

The Akashic Records

The Akashic records hold all the records of any and every life a soul has had. To me, it has always appeared as an immense cave looking library with floor-to-ceiling shelves of books and scrolls. Within these books and scrolls are described the elements of a soul's life experience, detailing events, people and places involved, thoughts and emotions held and actions taken.

The Akashic records have different facets to them being the stronghold of all known experience. They are connected to every single dimension, element, and soul. Aspects of it are well guarded. No one soul is able to ever destroy it. It contains the ultimate self's DNA, if you will. In the realm of the afterlife, the Akashic records are mostly a place of knowledge and understanding, and being able to access them is a privileged moment. Every spirit I have communicated with has said that not everyone gets to see their Akashic record when they want. To be allowed access demands reason in the growth of souls. Soul purpose is taken very seriously in the afterlife! If the query doesn't match the purpose of the soul's intent, there is no going in.

A guardian guards the room. To some he is stern, challenging, cross-armed, and imposing. To me he sometimes appears as this little chief gnome. He is hilarious! Yes, challenging, and no, if your reason for access isn't good enough, you can't come in. Souls wanting to enter the Akashic records always have to ask. They may be refused entrance. Once inside, the walls of records go on and on. Their lines, corridors, and shelves stretch as far as you can see. The guardian makes his way through, leading you to your answer, sometimes using mechanics or magic to take you there. You may experience elevators, buttons, and ladders. You may see your guardian fly through the air as he gets you your book or scroll. A page of a book opens up before you and you get to read your answer right there and then. Be quick. Trust. Read and know you will remember.

Just like within the temple, the Akashic records contain crystals within it for its record keeping. Some souls may enjoy exploring them for historical topics of lives in different worlds, or to access past lives of their own for better understanding. Crystals will show you names, dates, and connections to people and situations. It's really cool! These crystals are huge. They stand in the center lighting up the entire space and souls gather around screening their facets for information related to their query. They may not be touched. The question asked and the soul's vibrational presence bring forth through them the information requested, which is then downloaded into the consciousness of the soul. No extra information other than the specific answer to the querent's question can be read or downloaded. You may see that there's more information to be had, for instance, a paragraph before the one you can read on a scroll, but you are not able to read it. With Akashic records, questions are answered with precision, and accordingly to the soul's truest intent. Connected to the Akashic records is the wall of threads and the door to the future.

The Wall of Threads

The wall of threads represents all the threads of life of all souls past and present. Past, present and future lives are threaded together in an ever-lasting tapestry of vibrant colors. Its purpose is to show the connections between lives, particularly the vibrational level of consciousness within each one. Each life has its vibrational light; a color associated to the frequencies of the state of consciousness the soul enters to experience life. A thread of a specific life may have different hues of the same color, and may even change should the level of consciousness of the soul change during that time. As life continues in the afterlife, the colors also change as the soul journeys through the different vibrational levels thereon.

When you approach the wall of threads, what seems like a dull wall turns to … drum roll … a wall of threads! Literally. Changing colors as they go, on and on and on, you find threads one within another, on top, below, some tight, some loose, sometimes with many intertwined in between. It's a glowing show of the threads of life and it's amazing.

Before the wall stands a guardian. Again, it's a checkpoint. Once the query accepted, the guardian takes you straight to that part of your thread you question, and then it's up to you to see within it. The guardian does not help in translation. He stays quietly by your side until you are done contemplating.

Within the threads are our blueprints and what we made of them in our experiences of life. One after another, the timeline of our lives as a soul can be explored. A soul zooms into the part of the thread shown and can revisit parts of the blueprint it once had or is having now. The soul may see that there are future threads associated to the one presented, but it is nearly impossible for a soul to access these, as its purpose in life resides in the current one experienced. To visit threads pertaining to the future, the soul would need to be a time-travelling soul with a mission and a purpose to be, related to future events. Souls that engage in time travel may check on future threads pertaining to that which it is currently experiencing to resolve issues or to confirm it stays on track with its current mission in life.

Some threads on the wall have short spouts of color followed by lengthier ones. This may indicate short life spans amidst lengthier ones, or sudden changes in consciousness. Upon closer inspection, the soul may view the lifespan of the blueprints and its details, which lie within his thread, to know the difference. When a thread is crystal clear or transparent white, it indicates a soul experience of great enlightenment. The clearer the thread, the more enlightened the soul. Threads that intertwine with other threads indicate a non-linear experience of time and interconnection with others. When a thread intertwines with others and is also clearer than those around, it is a sign that the soul is more enlightened, is one with many and probably has a mission to expand greater awareness.

When a soul transitions to the afterlife, the blueprint ends but the thread continues. The color of the thread of a soul entering the afterlife may vary according to the soul's level of consciousness. The darker the thread, the denser in vibration it goes. Some parts of a soul's thread may show dots. These symbolize the short timespans the soul experienced itself as dense matter. In fact, at the beginning of the wall of thread I am told it looks more like a vast ball dotted with tiny spots. The only way I can think of explaining this is that at the beginning, there was soul consciousness, but one that looked chaotic, all over the place, with dots of singular experiences everywhere that eventually co-created the timelines seen on the wall of threads. To know for sure, I guess time will tell.

One of the most amazing messages I have received in regards to these threads is that, when contemplated, the thread may only show the current situation, as it stands in relationship to the soul's "now", but this can have consequences to the soul's future experiences. The result of that contemplation can not only change the future, but also the past, as vibrational intent in that moment connects the soul to all parts of its thread, past, present and future. As a soul in the afterlife contemplates on its thread, it is immediately influencing that very thread throughout, just as a drop would send ripples in the ocean that it is a part of. Therein lies the true power of the wall of threads; soul contemplation changes all.

The Door to the Future

The door to the future can come from many directions, one of which from the Temple of Knowledge. From the temple, stairs lead a seeking soul to the basement, leading it through its past. Ironically, the soul's journey toward the future entails a certain awareness of its past experiences. A soul desiring of seeking its future must consider where it comes from and what it takes to break the barriers of change for future experiences. For what the future holds, there is always change first. A thought, a desire, an idea; all hold moments of change. Even the desire to go to the future holds an idea of change. What may lie ahead? What's next? Souls in the afterlife ask themselves the same questions and seek answers through available sources of knowledge.

The door to the future is opened mostly, souls say, by the force of hope. Hope is a very strong co-creative force for souls. It brings together co-creative friends to help build a dream future. It gives stronger meaning to the experiences to come. It offers the strength to be, with a purpose and a reason to find. With hope, souls may gain insights into future events and relationships by visiting the door to the future. Once down the stairs, there are in fact three doors, the door back to the present, the door into the past and the door to the future. The soul having descended the stairs toward these doors has had to face certain current fears, nagging thoughts, hard-wired beliefs and expectations related to past experiences. Reaching the basement level to the doors can be slow, depending on the intent of the soul's desire to reach its goal and the time it wants to dwell on the journey of past events. Should a soul ignore related past moments, the flight of stairs can be short, but then again, the door to the future may not open due to the fact that the soul may not be well enough prepared to walk through.

Once at the bottom of the stairs, the door to the future faces the soul. It is shut. The other two doors are not. The door to the future is closed and has a shutter at the level of the third eye, which lies in the middle of the forehead. The shutter appears to have a question mark on it; a sign to ask the right question, a hint to the soul to use wisdom when asking about the future. Whatever the question, future-seeking souls will then be able to explore potentialities and possible opportunities, related to the vibrational offering they give as they stand before the door.

The one suggestion I have before opening the door to the future is to desire and expect the best. When a soul faces the door with as much faith, hope, and expectancy as possible, it will see its greatest desires met beyond and will better understand how to align to them from where it stands. The door to the future can show the best of what may be, but can also offer potentials of the worst depending on the patterns of life and the vibrational offerings the soul presents itself with.

Afterlife Soul Awakening

What does a soul do in the afterlife? I mean, granted it lives in bliss, (or hell, or something in between), and acknowledging a soul still has the ability for mental pursuit and self-purpose, what "happens"? Are they confronted to situations like we do in reality, or dreams? Do they have to adapt to the environment, or are they blasted into space where, if not they, who decides?

They reminded me we live in a mathematical multiverse. Mathematics, our language of creation, has come up with the fact that multiple universes exist. They added the memory of our mind power. Talking with soul consciousness, I went crazy over the potentials of perspectives I was presented, and which ones to choose from. One minute I truly believed I was talking to the dead, and the next I am questioning quantum physics. It's not easy believing in what others may not believe in. Souls have told me that believing in what others may not is exactly what they live with all the time. Even in time in the afterlife. The experience of self in the afterlife never ceases to be. As souls, we seem to always be seeking more of ourselves, no matter what. The only difference is how we live it and what we become, share and co-create of it. Like the rays of the sun, we are living to extend ourselves.

There are levels in the afterlife which may include, or not, time. In the moments time exists, the journey has its reason to be. In the zones of no-time, there is more an experience of thought without consequence. A dismissal of alignments during which co-creation may happen. It's like having an idea that nothing follows through with. Souls in the afterlife do! It's all recorded. They all take and have stake in what happens. They do this because love is their essence. Souls in the afterlife, wherever they be, are acting out a moment of love. Love is the one thing that permeates all, and it has many facets! Not all of them are easy to face. Take the soul that initiated war and death on Earth. What went through that aspect of love? Or the soul that decided to terminate its death in front of a loved one? What consequences of love do we experience from soul decisions? Some would say there is no love in that, and guess what? That's exactly what our Brilliant Essence explores. Places where love seems absent are spaces souls explore. A husband that does not act as expected, a child that does the abominable through pain, a rejection of loving understanding that brings unemployment or illness. And so it is also in the afterlife.

The soul that seeks a better experience and manifestation of love participates in such endeavors in the afterlife. It will strive to use its known resources, it's understanding of co-creation and it's drive to better be to bring forth its best experience of love. As it finds itself as it is, where it is in the afterlife, its core self will strive to better be. The soul takes stand as to where it is, what and who it may be, and relates to, and goes from there. I asked about souls living who desire to embody a much higher self than the next one in another dimension; a soul that wants to encompass many more and become an archangel of sorts, or Christ-consciousness. These experiences of self, they responded, are those of the consciousness of ones who no longer have the need or desire to be so specific in and through love. It is not so much a desire of being one than that of encompassing more desires through which one exists. It is the one who is called to love more, in more ways than one. Now get this right; the ones we are, those that strive, that pain, that stretch, explore, test, fail and succeed, we are the ones at the boundaries of our selves, and hence at the boundaries of our ultimate Self. We are explorers, adventurers, painkillers and bliss discoverers! When a soul retrieves itself to an afterlife experience, its spirit (soul consciousness) can encompass much more than itself, many more than the ones it has split itself into. It can become singularity. It all depends on what that soul consciousness wants to align with and how it does so. The key is love. Love is at the source of all and any and every experience tells a soul how love flows. And this is what afterlife soul awakening is all about.

Reconnecting

When a soul passes into the afterlife, those left behind struggle with the loss and absence of their dear one gone. Some are lucky enough to be able to reconnect with ease while others believe their loved ones are gone forever and that reconnecting is impossible. All souls in the afterlife are capable of reconnecting with their loved ones. They use their understanding of energetic alignments, as one would use a freeway, to connect to this person or that. Departed souls explain that to communicate, both sides need to be in vibrational alignment. Even a small thought can allow for communication but may not be clear to both parties. Like fine-tuning to a radio station, our connections can vary.

Our greatest connection is that of love, and if we allow that loving back and forth to prime over our doubts, we can maintain steady streams of clear communication. Love is the primary vibrational alignment departed souls use to align with others. They reach out to the living driving their intent through the threads of love that connect us in hopes that our state of consciousness allows for the receiving and the giving. When we are in a state of meditation, a dream state or one of mental relaxation, it is easier for us to receive. Our state of relaxation allows for our sensorial perceptions to be open to the non-physical and the information that flows within. As we let go of our habitual physical perceptions of life, we can invite our extra-sensorial perceptions to kick in and deliver to our consciousness that which we cannot normally see, hear or feel. With an open mind and an open heart, reconnection is made easier.

If we happen to be in lower vibrations in mind and heart, we may struggle to reconnect with loved ones passed who are in higher dimensions, and instead may find ourselves connecting with entities in lower vibrations, where states of consciousness are similar to the ones we offer. Departed souls know the alignments we live with here. They know we use our five senses to connect amongst ourselves. They know the mental blocks we may be dealing with. They maneuver around belief patterns, sensory systems and energetic fields to connect and communicate with the living. They work with us to create an interpretable, comprehensible language for better understanding and validation that it is in fact them who are contacting us. Some souls have very strong ties to the material world. These souls can push books off shelves, play with electricity, or yell in our ears. They use the frequencies closest to our sense of reality: sound, scent, touch, and sight. They can manipulate matter within those vibrational alignments to show up, be heard, and be felt, seen, and smelled. These are the signs to watch out for, especially at the time of death of a loved one when these alignments are the strongest.

Like with all languages, communicating with the departed needs to be tested and practiced. Souls will continue to test their transmission just as we receivers should too. When we call out in despair, with negative feelings or thoughts attached, who knows what soul connects first to that vibration. However, when we cry out and feel the love we have for the departed soul, it responds in like vibration and missing a loved one can translate to that loved one reaching out to you and letting you know how much you are loved. In fact, souls have said that the power of love expressed in grief is as close as it gets to the intensity of love our departed ones have for us on the other side. In those moments, we get a brief sensation of how much we are truly loved. Our guides encourage us to connect with peace of heart, a relaxed and open mind, and as much loving intent as possible.

Souls departed reconnect in various ways and from various places. Some souls remain so close to our reality, they may appear right beside us, day or night. Other souls, having moved on and disconnected with the realm of life on Earth, may need an in between space where the connection is helped. These spaces of reconnection may look and be experienced quite differently from one soul to another, but the common field of observation ties them together and makes this energetic field a complex multidimensional reality within which souls may navigate. One of the places where souls gather to reconnect in the afterlife looks like a massive room with huge glass globes through which life on Earth can be observed. Like a high-tech machine, a globe can zone in on a situation or person of interest. Elsewhere, souls are able to enter back into our space and time to reconnect by aligning to objects or elements of nature present on Earth. These souls connect or reconnect to our reality by bringing themselves into the chosen dimension in spirit using the form offered, like using a vessel to pour their intent. Children are particularly good at finding these soul appearances as they allow for souls to speak to them without condition. Dolls and teddy bears are notorious for holding such spaces for souls to communicate through.

Once a soul finds a way to reconnect with their dear one alive, they will keep repeating the process. The connection may come at a specific time, with a specific perfume or the same feeling of a hand on the shoulder. It could come as the same song repeated over and over again, or the same picture that keeps moving on a wall. My dad and I always meet on the same beach. Mother Mary always comes with the same scent. Archangels are often tied to specific colors so they may appear through hues of that color. Monarch butterflies are said to hold the spirit of the departed and many have said having used one to make their presence known. As soon as souls get a "hit" with the consciousness of those alive, they will repeat the process to validate and grow the reconnection.

Preparing for Rebirth

Reincarnation is now widely accepted as a potential for new experiences of life. Although not all souls choose to reincarnate, stories abound today of the living remembering a recent past life. In the afterlife, reincarnation is taken very seriously and preparation is key, the first one being the reason. Souls in the afterlife choose to be reborn for various reasons, for example, souls having left this world abruptly may want to come back to finish what they had started in their previous life. Cases of near-death experiences report that souls choose to come back to life to continue what they came here to do. Should a soul not be able to regain the body it left, it will be reborn shortly thereafter to pursue its goals. Souls may also desire to balance out a karmic debt or an experience of opposites; once a killer, now a savior, once rich, now poor, once a woman, now a man. Children having stronger awareness of their most recent experiences in life, including experiences in the afterlife, tell how they used to be a boy and now chose to be a girl, or how they used to be a mother in the family it is now reborn as a grandchild of.

Some souls travel to other worlds or rebirth in different forms. Asked if a soul can be reborn as an animal or a plant, the answer is yes. To my experience, a soul rarely reports having gone from being human to being a tree, but since time is relative, and anything and everything is possible, why not? After all, it must surely depend on the soul's intention to be. Souls say that in the greater scheme of existence, balance is sought in relationship to expansion and evolution of all that is and a soul's life will reflect this through its desire to be.

As the soul prepares to re-enter the form of a human, it goes through a series of steps to be able to engage itself in this reduced form of being. Take the Russian doll analogy of the greater soul desiring to experience itself as a smaller version of itself within itself. It must decide what version of itself it desires to encompass, the aspects of itself it wants to experience, its form, conditions, its reason to be, goals to reach, place of existence, connections to others, etc. Preparing for rebirth is as complex and exciting as can be.

Souls that have cycled through the afterlife and are desiring of a new experience of themselves go through moments of death. The unwanted is recycled and the desires are brought to creation, changing the direction of the soul's experience. When a soul desires to let go of certain aspects of itself, certain habits or certain relationships, it goes through the process of evaluation, potentiality and possibility. The soul basically asks itself what it really wants, what it has to further its desires and what drives it to move forward. It's like asking yourself if your old car is good enough for the trip you want to take. If not, what would you rather have and if you have it, what would you do with it. Souls who have the thought to reincarnate on Earth ask themselves the same questions and then decide what alignments to keep and which ones they will do without.

Reincarnation for these souls may be as prepared as possible, but always comes with a shock. The liberation of what was to what is when done is always abrupt in the moment. Either we accept it, or we don't. If we accept it, liberation turns to pleasure and interest in what is new. If we don't accept it, we often fall back to old patterns, wherein the soul must accept itself within. The aware soul may still linger in thought to what has been, whilst discovering a new experience. A little like when a mom remembers her son as a baby, and yet sees the man she has in front of her. A mother always knows when a separation to her child may come. It is their soul agreement coming back to light to alleviate the pain in the moment and to make it more one of wonder, as was meant to be.

As a soul reaches to go beyond what it has gained in the afterlife, many words and dimensions of consciousness may be explored and spirit (soul consciousness) always seeks. A soul always wants love, pleasure, happiness, well-being and purpose. It wants to be in the best of ways. Souls sometimes forget they came into their experiences with limitations to breakthrough, to overcome to better be. It is the experiences of such moments that give them drive as they see that they are not alone in so being and doing. They see other souls suffering the same way, or even more. They want to make a difference in how they feel and witness others being. To make a difference, souls accept to be different, whilst relating, and to relate, one must care for their presence and absence. One must understand the power of being a soul.

Dying is believing, I once heard a soul say. Where's the fun in that, I asked. Laughing, enjoying life are elements of certain states of consciousness, it responded. Ask your mind to seek the fun and joy. Align yourself to laughter. Let change speak for itself. When we prepare for rebirth, reincarnation, or any change for ourselves, we do it with thought as to what we wish to experience more of. Let that be your motivation for change and allow for those who change to move forward, knowing they will always be with you, no matter what.

The Blueprint—Part 1

The blueprint is the soul's signature map to the experience ahead.

It is not set in stone, but some parts are unchangeable. The blueprint serves to

- choose our families to be born into
- choose the cellular memories to carry
- choose our physical and mental conditioning
- choose where to place our karmic debt
- choose which skills to come in with and which ones to enhance
- choose where on the blueprint to place signals to pay attention to or to recognize
- choose which relationships to entertain
- choose who helps and who to help
- choose the possibilities of death and the potential times of death

The blueprint is always revised with the help of master guides.

Master Guides

Master guides are souls who are beyond the scope of consciousness and awareness of those they guide. Because they are as much aligned with the highest as with the lowest, their point of balance is where they stand and the scope of reach is what they may offer in guidance. A master guide lives its experience of life in a different plane than that of the souls it serves, and may take different forms holding the vibrational level of consciousness it has. If they so choose, when they appear to the student soul, the form they appear with is as much a part of the guidance as the message they deliver.

A meeting with master guides always happens before a soul is reborn. During this meeting, the blueprint is reviewed and the soul has a chance to discuss their choice of life. Blueprints are not set in stone. Everything on the blueprint relates first and foremost to where the soul is before coming to life, what state it wants to evolve to, and how it chooses to do so. Any experience that evolves the soul is calculated and planned for ahead, with all known potentials exposed. This is why the guidance of masters is important, as they have a greater scope of understanding as to what may be. You have to understand, these guys are great–great masters, great souls who love to live and laugh all the time, through us all, no less. When a master comes to you, you are really with one of your great higher selves. They will never quit on you. Master guides love you more than you know. Master guides lovingly recognize that it is through you that expansion happens, which is why the blueprint is not set in stone. Without the freedom of will, there would be no new discovery of self to explore. Our free will allows for the soul to venture into new horizons of self. Our free will allows for new experiences and new perspectives in life. Master guides always let free will be. They are there to check on us before we blunder off.

The meeting is impressive. A soul can reunite with them in life (via meditation) as in death, and the meeting will still impress by their presence alone. They personify the greater levels of consciousness of souls. These are direct soul consciousness descendants of you, in vibrational alignment to you, and may come through the forms of beings of light, angels, or friends and family to help you on your journey. At the meeting, reviewing your blueprint, they may also be present.

The number of master guides at the meeting differs from one soul to another. Master guides hold the meeting to assure the potential for the chosen blueprint to work, a little like a parent asking the kid to tie his shoelaces before running off. The meeting usually takes place in an empty yet imposing space. There is nothing to distract and everything to respect. Master guides will appear in vibrational alignment to the soul with distinction of higher knowingness.

During the meeting, items of the blueprint are discussed. The blueprint is not challenged. What are discussed are the desired outcomes the soul rebirthing wants from the experience. Are the goals too tall an order? How many chances does one have to get it right? When can the soul reevaluate, change or accelerate its course? What if an accident happens from the evolvement of free will? Which part of the soul wants to grow and which part of its current alignments does it want to keep? What if the soul's consciousness digresses in the process? What then?

All these questions involve the soul at many more levels than one, and masters make sure the reborn soul knows where it is going and for what purpose. They also make sure the soul always keeps a connection to its higher aspects of self no matter what. Luckily, blueprints create predefined conditions and alignments. So to stray beyond the soul's well-being that it was born to live really needs heavy lifting to happen. Masters point out where those moments may be, and their signaled presence is measured in the picture. Warning signs, curveballs, a chance encounter—these are the moments your highest self is signaling you to pay attention to and to know you are not alone.

At the meeting, master guides are distinct and recognizable not by name but by behavior, voice, and perception. One guide will exude the deepest love and compassion a soul can resonate to, aligned with the likes of Mother Mary and Buddha. Another will bring a sensation of deep strength and purpose, associated perhaps to Archangel Michael or the prophet Mohamed. When a soul aligns to its master guide, their specific gifts and purpose are exchanged to guide the soul to greater consciousness.

The Blueprint—Part 2

The blueprint maps out the life to come of a soul. Each life has its blueprint. Between blueprints is what the soul lives in the afterlife. The afterlife is a blank canvas where free will is absolute. Blueprints condense this free will to conditions and alignments of desires. This creates purpose and goal. Throughout the blueprint, the purpose and goals of a soul are sought, and preconditions within the blueprint help their fulfillment. Blueprints may or may not hold elements of surprise. Free will is maintained and surprises desired or not, can happen. Even blueprints may end abruptly by surprise. Sometimes a soul is thrown back into life to finish what it didn't. "God said I had to come back, and I came back instantly," I heard someone say who had just encountered a near-death experience. Whichever way the blueprint was meant to end, what comes as a surprise is always taken into consideration within the blueprint.

Blueprints are based on evaluated potentiality. Their content is much like a string of risk verses gain with lots of colored elements of life to it. They include states of consciousness, points of validation, cities to be in, people to meet, growth potential and turnkey events and interconnect with the blueprints of others in the process. They also include options to leave the body. When I was a child, I knew I had many chances to leave my body and return to the afterlife. I somehow knew this was part of my blueprint options. When I failed to die after trying to commit suicide, I knew I had to give up one chance to stay alive, and I have had three narrow escapes before, but my will to survive had me live. Life is not a joke, they say in the afterlife. If you want to throw it away, let another one take your place. Sometimes souls do just that. Walk-ins, for example, are souls who take over a still-able body when another soul has done its time. This is written as an option in both blueprints, that of the soul leaving the body and that of the one entering it. Other options may involve alternate realities according to the soul's growth in consciousness. A soul having gone beyond the point of consciousness its blueprint offered in a still-able body may live its free will to pursue beyond it. These souls experience a heightened sense of self and may experience the luxury of living their greater selves within the scope of a third dimensional body.

The blueprint is carefully sketched out by the incoming soul who determines what alignments and goals it desires to experience in life. Souls desiring to live a human experience align their blueprint to humankind and an era of life on Earth or on another planet. These conditions reduce greatly the scope of free will it may have in the afterlife, limiting it as a social co-creator to a specific space and time it wants to be a part of. The soul's aptitudes and goals are fashioned around its purpose to be. Its purpose to be is predefined. Its purpose to be relies on the elements of a blueprint to be realized. Throughout the blueprint, the soul's purpose is reminded to the incarnated one. Signals that a soul is on track are placed therein. Options and spaces for greater free will are also included. The blueprint doesn't tell what a soul will live. It cannot guarantee a certain experience of life. It can only suggest. It is up to the soul to experience the map as it goes and to make of it what it will. Sometimes a soul may have a really tough time living certain aspects of its blueprint and this is where our higher selves and guides come in to help. Other times a soul is impatient to move along finding its chosen time and space too restrictive for its level of awareness. The soul's higher self and consciousness then take over the restricted space the blueprint offered, allowing expansion of the soul's experience to be in greater ways. The blueprint helps the soul guide itself through life, where will power and change make a mark but it's the soul's free will that makes life what it is.

Blueprints are created with timing in mind. They are not created in the same time-space as the time-space the life is to be. They are created beyond time where time does not exist other than in the experience of the moment of creation. Blueprints are held in a timeless space where only the point of observation gives it time. The blueprint of a child to be born may be created "at the same time" as that of its mother to be. The mother-to-be may have created her blueprint at a time where motherhood didn't even exist. The blueprint is based on the level of awareness of a soul at any given time and its desire to be accordingly. It is a statement in time.

The Hall Meeting

After meeting with the masters, and the blueprint finished, the time is near to leave. A big reunion is held inviting all the souls involved to join the one leaving. The one leaving has had practice focusing elsewhere. It has made agreements with everyone to meet up and to play the game of life. It is ready to focus its consciousness into a human body and mind. It is excited for what is to come, and so are its soul friends. This reunion is one of celebration, goodwill, and good fortune bestowed upon the birthing soul.

Some of these souls will be only temporarily met in the new life. Others will be life long partners. All connected souls are invited to the hall meeting. The hall is huge. It can hold thousands. The soul is greeted with cheers from its friends, certain life elements flashing before them. Some souls present have already been reborn, yet their higher selves make their presence known. Other souls may birth after and come to rejoice the future shared experience. It's a party. Most of them appear in their human or earthly forms. Yes, there are animals, insects, and birds at the gathering too. If a pet were to be in the next life, the soul of that pet would appear at the gathering with recognizable aspects to it that the soul would click with in its future. These aspects tell the nature of the relationship the soul will have to them. Nature souls are often healers and helpers in disguise. Birds tell, insects remind, animals balance.

Some souls will show themselves with traits to signal, such as a future husband. When a soul is reborn, it does not remember whom it is to marry, but it will flash at the right person at the right time because of this inner signal. It will flash on a puppy to save, or a bird that keeps coming around for good fortune. These flashes will trigger the soul's memory to validate the blueprint's path. Signals are induced vibrational triggers that the soul carries through its alignments into life. Signals can take the form of a gut feeling, a sudden burst of joy, an eye-catching moment, a synchronicity, or a coincidence. A signal to something important directly related to a blueprint moment will be noticed by the soul. It's up to the soul to act upon it. The meeting helps consolidate it. The hall meeting is the last time the soul will see his friends on this side within the same vibration. This is the transitioning out of the afterlife consciousness into a new experience of growth through life. This growth starts in the mother's womb.

In the Mother's Womb

The soul doesn't settle in its new body instantly. Some souls come in and out throughout the process of pregnancy. Souls have told me they will not settle in before the first three weeks of pregnancy are over. Incoming souls need to adapt to their new conditions, and even in the womb, conditions may change and disrupt the journey into birth. Remember, souls come in with excitement. They come in happy and full of love. Life is an opportunity based on love, and this holds true for all souls reborn. In the womb, the soul connects more and more to the conditions matching its blueprint. Its place of consciousness is focused into its new experience in mind and body.

The attachment to the mother is fast but not guaranteed. A mother who aborts before the three weeks may not experience a soul connection at all with the rejected fetus even though a soul may have tried to birth. If the woman loses her baby after three weeks, for whatever reason, she has a stronger connection with the soul that didn't make it through because of the greater link in physicality they both had. All mothers will recognize in the afterlife the soul they nearly birthed. The soul that went through the process with you will always be with you.

When pregnant, a mother has the growing body within her to preoccupy her mind, but she can also feel it when the soul's spirit comes in and out. It is her duty to guarantee safe haven for the soul. The calmer the environment, the happier the soul is to stay. A pregnant woman can practice checking in with her baby by paying attention to the signals she receives, either in mind or through emotional and physical reactions. I remember going to Hawaii seven months pregnant only to find that my baby did not enjoy being underwater. Personality does not take long to implement, and an aware mother may connect and ready herself in advance with the incoming soul. Meditation brings a huge advantage for parents-to-be. Honing in and inviting a soul connection through meditation is very easy, and with practice, the mother can actually follow the child through the birthing canal and know exactly when to push and where (which, by the way, should be taught more!).

The incoming soul experiences any and all connections to its parents-to-be as it prepares to face the realities of these alignments once born. Should the mother have a sudden emotional reaction, the baby will be affected by it immediately, sometimes to such an extent, especially in early pregnancy, that it disconnects completely and goes straight back into the afterlife. After a significant disruption while in the womb, the birthing soul may leave and be replaced by another. This may sound shocking, but the aware mother will feel this and adamantly tell the story that she has a different baby in her womb. Souls in the afterlife help each other just as they do here, and should a mother truly want a child, she is a potential incubator for not just one but other souls lined up to come. In the mother's womb starts the soul's journey through life on Earth. Do they really know what they are in for?

After the Afterlife

When souls decide to be born as humans, they are not thrown into a body and left to manage. They come in with predetermined alignments, some of which they have had, time and time again, in birth and rebirths. These alignments change as the soul evolves. Alignment after alignment is what the soul experiences of itself. Each alignment brings the soul to a new understanding of self. Birthing as a baby is an opportunity for the evolving soul to grow through life on Earth.

Not all souls want to step into a life experience on Earth. Some would simply prefer to watch, observe, study, and grow in other ways, with perhaps good reason! Souls can be and become absolutely anything they set themselves to experience. Every soul consciousness knows how true this is and always has something in its path set as a reminder that anything and everything is possible and that it can do absolutely anything and everything it sets itself to experience. This inner knowingness lies within the strength of hope. Hope doesn't come from wishful thinking. Hope comes from this inner knowingness that the soul can accomplish whatever it wants. Hope as a thought, may die, but the knowingness that the soul can and may do as it desires, does not! Some rebirth, others stay where they are in the afterlife, others yet move to other forms and states of being. Anything and everything is possible. After the afterlife begins a new experience in more dimensions than one. Which ones are real and which ones are still ideas to only one? This I cannot answer. All I can say is that from the many aspects of souls I have encountered, reality seems greater than fiction!

To conclude on the soul's journey from death to rebirth, it is clear to me we have more to live than life itself. Reality isn't always what it seems. Mine is greater than I can tell. I'm pretty sure yours is too.

PART 2

Questions and Answers from Spirit

Where there is life, there is love.

Experiencing Death

Channeling is the art of tuning into a soul's vibration and allowing for communication to happen through you as a medium. Following are channeled communications between myself and souls past who have lived a life on Earth. As you will see, I am sometimes skeptical as to what happens when I channel, but I thought it would be a good idea to share with you examples of these discussions that have lead me to better understand life after death. I name the channeled soul Spirit unless otherwise indicated.

Spirit: I was an atheist and died of a heart attack.

Astrid: What happened next?

Spirit: I felt intense pain, and soon after that I was engulfed in a white light. I felt fully conscious, but at the same time I felt the jolt of my coming out of my body. I felt I was floating, and I thought I was in a coma. It seemed like the logical explanation. Then, like in a dream, I started seeing familiar faces, like on the sides of the wall of a tunnel I was going through. They were smiling. I remember thinking, *Why am I seeing you?*

At that point, I remembered what I had heard about near-death experiences and the tunnel of light they referred to, but at the time I had thought it a good premise to a movie at best. I was brought up without faith. I became a scientist. Nothing about my life was reproducible. At least I fought to prove it.

Like in a split-personality moment, part of me was in wonder of my experience while the other part of me was trying to connect it with what I thought I knew. My mind was still alive! That's when I noticed that regardless of what I thought of myself, I had no body to respond with. I could sense myself, but I could not see it. When I looked down at my arms, they were nothing but fuzzy ideas of what they could look like. My legs, which seemed to float under me, were unresponsive to my desire to move them.

I felt surrounded by intense light. Not quite white, not quite transparent, not quite thick, this light that started off as a spark in the distance was closing in. At first I thought it might be a being of sorts—an angel or an alien. A tiny thought came up: *Well, should I be thinking of God or death right now?* However, it was like the rest of my thoughts, just passing thoughts as if my consciousness was grasping at threads of past thoughts just to stabilize.

By the time I was immersed in the white light I was wide-awake. Confused, I asked, "What is this? I know I am here and not on Earth. So what's next?" Immediately my consciousness went to thinking mind over matter: *I want out and refuse to be here.* What was light turned to dark. Space caved in. I had the strongest feeling that if I didn't change my mind, I'd find myself in a holding cage.

Just like in the movies. I calmed myself and allowed for space to be.

Things opened up again, and the white light became more prominent again. Part of me was interrogating this mind manipulation, while the other part was acknowledging, experiencing, and testing it out. Time was of no essence, only a thought. What mattered was where I was, what I was doing there, and what was next.

Astrid: What happened next?

Spirit: Out of the mist of white people came toward me. Everyone I had seen on the walls of the tunnels was there with beings I felt I knew but did not recognize. My heart jolted back to those I knew I was leaving behind, and I plummeted back into the dark. Many times afterward I have had to experience this feeling of plummeting back down. It is not a pleasant feeling when out of control.

People came from all sides toward me, some with smiles, some without. But everyone who didn't have a facial expression glowed of love. At that point I finally admitted to the existence of auras.

I don't know how, but their presence seemed to have an irreversible impact on my way of thinking. It was as if, all at the same time, I knew I was dead, I knew I had transitioned, I knew I was with my loved ones, I knew my life was behind me, and most of all, I understood it was all just a dream. Life, death. Just a dream. Not fully recognized, yet the thought was real. I had awakened to a new dream state.

Astrid: What is the last thing you remember feeling about your body?

Spirit: My legs. It was as if they were dematerializing. I had the sensation of having them yet I knew they were no longer there. I wasn't in the skin anymore, but I did feel the outer layers connected to space. Like what people with amputations would feel about their missing limbs.

Astrid: Why do you call your state of being a dream state?

Spirit: So you can relate to it in the most empowering way. Here we get to understand the principles and powers of connections. We realize what connections we had and what they led up to. We are also well aware of the potentiality of our current connections, so the more inspiring we are to you, the better for you.

Astrid: Some would call that manipulation of mind or imagination. How can we trust that what you say is real?

Spirit: Watch a movie that takes place in the future, and you will see something that hasn't happened yet and may never happen. Listen to the experience of someone who fought in a war, gave birth to a child, or just fell in love and your perspective will change. Experiences may be shared in a variety of ways that only the listener gets to hear at his own accord. Whatever resonates with you shall. The rest will be forgotten and left to others, if any. All experiences have a lifespan and are recorded.

Astrid: Where are you now, and what do you do?

Spirit: I am in a form of utopia, if you will. We do not have days. Our time is experienced through passages of thought rather than passages or cycles of time. Our thoughts lead us to another that leads us to another while through them we visit and experience aspects of ourselves within them. This is why I call it a dream state, because just like in dreams you have on Earth, we live aspects of ourselves through moments of thought. In those we travel and we team up to explore common connections and interests. We live in a different time and space that isn't that far from yours. We are all connected!

Does Religion Matter?

Astrid: A Jew (J), a Muslim (M), and an atheist meet at the gates of heaven. Who goes in and who stays out?

J: I'm here—shalom.

Astrid: (he said something else but it was gibberish to me, so I stuck to what I understood) Hi. Thank you for speaking as clearly in English as is possible to share with us. So does this mean you consider yourself Jewish in the afterlife?

J: Oh, certainly. One of the perks of having passed over with a religion is to be able to keep the attachments of faith that you acquire through it.

Astrid: I see.

Atheist: Hi, I'm here.

Astrid: Your energy is quite different, clearer actually than that of J. It is emptier in a sense, like more transparent. Could you explain to us why that may be? Oh, and what's your name?

Atheist: Claude. I am glad you can distinguish our energy fields. We step forth with the weight, if you will, of our past faith so you can better interpret your answer. For me, religion had no weight on my transition. I did wonder in the past if I should or shouldn't before I die, but I died a pleasant death and was engulfed in the light very fast. I would say it is only in the aftermath that I had a bit of confusion as to what to think and where to go. There was no God who came to me. Loved ones, yes. Bliss and light, yes, immediately. But no Jesus, no God. Although they do exist.

Astrid: Ah, so you are no longer an Atheist.

Claude: Not in the sense you understand the word. I have God with me, in me and through me, as you know we all do. I just never called it God. And I still do not.

Astrid: What do you call it?

Claude: Essence.

Astrid: Oh cool. I call it Brilliant Essence!

Claude: Yes, fitting.

Astrid: I'm feeling our Muslim friend around.

M: Inch'Allah!

Astrid: Hi, how are you?

M: Great!

Astrid: How would you like to answer the question?

M: Well, I obviously went in too. I died relying on my faith to take me to heaven, and that's what it did.

Astrid: So it really isn't about religion, per se, but more about where your inner faith guides you?

M: It doesn't really feel like it guides you more than it takes you. It's a powerful draw that just takes you places.

Astrid: So you are not in control when you die?

M: I was not. Some are. I was not. Like Claude, I got wooshed up.

Astrid: What about you, J?

J: No, my passing was not like you see Claude's or M's. A lengthier passing. Nothing to do with my faith or religion. Just more steps to take, I guess.

Astrid: You guess? I didn't know spirits guessed in the afterlife.

J: I just don't know exactly what their passing was like, so I can only guess.

Astrid: I see. So to get this straight, religion has no factor in the passing other than what the soul has acquired from it in terms of faith.

J, M, and C: Yes.

Astrid: We agree we are not talking about what the person did with his or her faith, because then it would be a different story, right?

C: The doing and the thinking are separate. At the gates of heaven, which is basically at the time of self-judgment, when a soul may go into the heavens, those with religious faiths may have present religion-based guides. Atheists like me enjoy the presence of physicists and the like.

Astrid: Do you have a message for those who have a hard time with their religious upbringing?

C: Keep faith in yourself. Have faith that you are a good soul seeking the best in all.

Meeting the Masters

Spirit: Meeting your masters doesn't come easy. You don't just wish it to happen and it happens. They have to come together, and they won't unless they all have stakes in the matter. This only happens rarely. When a soul reaches out to speak to its master selves, the master-self aspects of the soul get triggered, and the immediate response of that level of love often suffices to set help—without their presence—in motion.

So when a soul actually presents itself in front of its masters, the level at which the soul presents itself had better be up to par with the vibrational level at which the masters, together, come through. I knew when I met my masters, they represented my higher aspects. I also knew I wanted their help with my next life. I had chosen one that was on the verge of what I thought I was capable of, but this breakthrough could help me let go and move onto the next level.

Astrid: What was your goal?

Spirit: My goal was to get rid of all karma I had left on Earth.

Astrid: Doesn't karma always exist? Don't all our actions have repercussions?

Spirit: There are places and spaces to deal with karma. The Earth cycle I was going into was one of them. I wanted to let go of the karma I still had left on Earth when Earth was also karmically cleansing so I could benefit from, participate in, and help out during her karmic cleansing too.

Astrid: What was the purpose of meeting with your guides?

Spirit: My master and guides were actually quite supportive. My objectives seemed to be within reasonable potentiality and my goal was clear. What they questioned me about was the expansion I expected of myself through the process, and I have to admit, I had only really thought of clearing myself of karma and being of help in the process. They wondered if my goals were not stealing me away from where I wanted to go, as a soul. I admitted to taking that for granted. This complacency of thought was dearly tested during my life as I cleared much of my karma; I had helped many people, but I lost the will to live for myself and found myself fighting back for life a few times over.

Astrid: Why would you loose the desire to live if you cleared yourself of karma?

Spirit: I couldn't find a place to go to, to move forward with. I was pretty much done with myself. I had done what I came to do, and I just wanted to go home.

Astrid: What have you to say to a soul who seeks his or her masters in life?

Spirit: Seek no more! They are with you now and always. If you want to bring them to life in the moment, to help you out, remember their greatness and strive to align without plea to that which you already have within you. Even if it seems like a molecule compared to an ocean or continent, believe you are aligned in love and that when you truly need their presence as you desire it to be, you will already be with it, to witness, experience, and identify with. Bottom line is, as you ask, you shall receive. A love principle I have immensely enjoyed the benefits of, and so can you!

Astrid: Could you elaborate on your suggestion to "strive to align without plea to that which you already have within you"? Could you give us an example on how to do this?

Spirit: What you have within you is love. Love is at the heart of all that is. Love is what you have within you that holds things together and that drives co-creation. Bring your awareness of yourself to the love you have within you. When you plea for better, you are signaling to yourself that something is not as good as what you would like it to be, and you are asking for change. Change what you don't like and keep what you do. Do this for yourself, first. You are the one to make the change so that the love you have and the love you seek may come together in your reality, through your experience.

Love flows like water or air through the gaps of life. The flow is that of ease. It is easy for water to flow through cracks. It is as easy for love to flow through troubles and issues. Follow the flow of love and it will be easy for you to be in a better place. For example, when a child has a tantrum, it is because there is too much of a difference between what the child feels is good and what the child experiences. Facing the child with hardship will only worsen the situation. Instead, stand in your place of love, come down to his level, eye to eye, and redirect the child toward that which is more loving, offering options to think and act differently. This is done with peace of heart and ease of mind. No plea, no expectations, simply an offering of the love within you to engage the love within the child to find a better solution. Love connects with everything. Love heals all.

.

The Guardian

Spirit: I'm the guardian of the Akashic records. Of course I don't let everyone in. I've got a wall behind me, and unless it lets me through, you won't be able to either. You probably just realized the immensity of what lies behind us all. Let it be given to you that this has always been, and we are exploring it together.

But don't ever think the wall behind you is solid. It never is. It is full of knowledge, thought, and action, and it will always back you up.

Astrid: How does one reach you?

Guardian: It's not my business to know and I don't ask. Sure, sometimes an incoming soul will really intrigue me, and I will ask where this comes from, but the wall always answers me first. Incoming souls are more of an entertainment to me!

Astrid: You have a big ego!

Guardian: I do my duty well because of who I am.

Astrid: So what's your story? How did you end up here?

Guardian: If that is what you seek, I may allow you in to find for yourself.

Astrid: When do you not allow souls to come in?

Guardian: When judgment goes against it. Even doubt can hold judgment sufficient to not allow the answer to come in this way. The soul is sent back to find its answer otherwise. It's usually not as easy as it expected it to be.

Astrid: Are you always so short and direct in your answers?

Guardian: Yes.

Astrid: (At this point I'm struggling to continue the conversation and psychically yelling out at all you guys: please ask a question while I have him online!) Do some souls not have to go through you?

Guardian: Yes.

Astrid: Who?

Guardian: Those who are already within the walls.

Astrid: Makes sense. Has anyone ever outwitted you?

Guardian: Yes. You.

Astrid: Okay, so now you are speaking to me as if I was self-reflective and of course I can outwit myself. Otherwise I would be stagnant and so would everything else and that only exists in its own stagnant dying space, blah, blah, blah. So what's the purpose of your being such a smarty-pants, know it all and what have you really got to say?

Guardian: First of all, let's be straight—you called me.

Astrid: Sorry! I forgot.

Guardian: In terms of personality, it distinguishes us from each other, even in the afterlife. I like mine. It serves me well, and it does its job correctly. I tremendously enjoy myself and those who come to me. Yes, you too, of course! I do acknowledge the powers others see in my role, but judgment does not affect me. There is plenty of it in front and behind these walls.

Astrid: Why have a guardian guard a wall that can guard itself?

Guardian: to offer companionship in thought.

Astrid: Please explain.

Guardian: The number of answers that lie beyond this wall is infinite. The soul that asks has in mind certain perspectives and certain allowances to think differently. So as not to be confused by the infinite possibilities of thought that may appear to the asking soul, my presence offers recognition, validation and evaluation as to which answer fits best the soul in the moment.

Astrid: How does your presence help?

Guardian: I appear as one who may think the same way you do. The asking soul relates to me as one who has the same type of logic it comes in with. I help navigate through thoughts that the soul can assimilate. If I were to appear as a monster, the soul would align its thoughts with the idea of a monster. If I were to appear as a dog, the soul would align its thoughts to its experience of dogs. My presence engages the soul's thoughts to align with the potentialities its question and my appearance have to offer.

Astrid: Do you appear differently to different souls?

Guardian: Yes indeed.

Astrid: indeed, as "in deed"? You mean to say you have a deed, an action to have toward souls that come to the wall?

Guardian: that is what I mean. My presence is my deed. How I present myself is my chosen action for the betterment of the soul's understanding. That is my role as a Guardian.

At the Hall Meeting

Spirit: I had forgotten how amazing the hall meeting was. It truly is a party. Everyone I was to meet in the next life was there. Absolutely everyone. How can they all be there, you ask? Thousands of souls gathered together at one point in time to celebrate the new life of a soul. Commendable! It is real. I guess you only realize it when you accept it as part of your soul's moments in life. The thing is, when you reach that point of being as a soul, it does become difficult to express in words the immensity of your experience. And this is definitely one of those moments.

Thousands gather. At first I thought I was just going into a big hall with a few of the most important souls to be in the next life. I had met them all and knew they would bid me farewell. But the more I contemplated my next life, the more these aligned loving souls stepped forward and rejoiced in the promise of a great journey.

During the review of the blueprint, I had engaged with realignments of what may await. I had to revisit fear, anxiety, strength of will and such that I chose to engage in. And we did make soul agreements, my friends and I. But during the hall meeting, none of those ideas or thoughts came up. I was super excited and everyone was there to cheer me on. I knew where I was going, I knew what to do and I knew who would be with me. It was a chance of a lifetime, and we were all really looking forward to this experience.

Astrid: Does everyone go through the hall meeting?

Spirit: Yes. They have to. Even if they don't remember, they have to. It's a question of being connected. And that connection always stems from love and light. And that love and light always feeds itself first before being able to feed another outside of itself. It's one of the principles of love. The only difference is that some souls that return to birth leave that aspect to their greater self and do not carry that memory forward. They are either not ready for it or it is irrelevant to their continued progress of where they are.

Astrid: My daughter asks if you meet teddy bear souls.

Spirit: You do! Teddy bears are special places for spirits to help and guide the soul of a young child. A child who ignites this possibility within the toy will open doors for the spirit of a soul to come and live temporarily. Explain to your child that up in heaven, she chose to have a friend who came through the teddy bear to love and help, and ultimately, at a higher place in heaven, they are both one. This is one person who decided to experience life in two different ways and be friends for a while in the process.

Do Souls Eat, Sleep, Drink, and Smoke?

Astrid: (I've always had a fondness for sisters in robes. My cousin is one of them, and a few of us in the family have asked ourselves when we were younger, could this be our path? I was thinking of ghost sisters, those who stay behind in places close to our human density and lower vibrations, to help souls passing through. So I pulled up my list of questions and they hit on this one!)

Astrid: (Laughing) Do ghost sisters drink, smoke, eat, or sleep in the afterlife?

Spirit: We enjoy the gifts of heaven.

Astrid: I can imagine you all sitting at a table with a glass of wine and some delicious foods in front of you.

Spirit: Yes! We do have a lot of fun, and because we are so close to earthly alignments, it is quite easy for us to manifest these pleasures in our reality. We even have a sense of smell and taste!

Astrid: Wow, that is so cool! Eating whatever you want, whenever you want! Do you get fat?

Spirit: (laughing) No. We don't need to. We live as closely related to the ones we serve, without a body.

Because we were sisters in robes in our previous lives, we wanted to perpertrae our duty once on the other side. We found each other and continue here to help those on Earth in need, specifically the ones transitioning from death to the afterlife.

Astrid: Who might they be? Why do they need your help?

Spirit: They are often ones with religious backgrounds like that which we represent, but have had issues with it, such as powerful guilt, fear of not finding their loved ones on the other side, fear of letting go of the loved ones left behind.

Astrid: Do you have children lost that way?

Spirit: Yes. Most often the children we help have had a sudden death and are confused as to where there home is.

Astrid: Do some of you smoke? Smoking is supposed to be bad for you.

Spirit: Some of us enjoy the smoke. A change of perception, such as one given through smoke, can have us appear to the eyes of the living. We use these changes in air to come when needed. We do not have bodies to worry about, however, density alignments are always tricky to handle should a soul not be balanced in who and where it is.

Astrid: Are you saying that it is the smoke of others you enjoy?

Spirit: Yes and no. We do not like what the smoke does to the body but we do enjoy using it to come through. Mist, fog, darkness all are agents for us to come through with. Smoke is a derivative. Bonfire smoke is also great for us to dance around in.

Astrid: But do you smoke.

Spirit: Occasionally.

Astrid: What about eating and sleeping? Do you do those too? Do you have cycles where you are at?

Spirit: Yes. Where we are is what you might call an alternate reality to yours. It has similar cycles and rhythms of life. We are all, however, ethereal.

Astrid: So you don't bump into each other?

Spirit: No, although we can surprise each other by our presence. We use the flows of that which is between those on Earth and those in the afterlife. Where we are, we use the cycles and rhythms connected to what the transitioning soul in difficulty is used to. We match our vibrations to that of the soul in thought and then in action.

Astrid: So you are basically living in limbo like the lost souls you help?

Spirit: You could call it that. We are not in limbo but you understand that they may be, so yes, in a sense. We are free to come and go. Our purpose is to help other souls do the same; to go further into the light where they may live in peace. So for that reason, we enjoy the pleasures of places in limbo whilst serving the love we come from and we maintain the energies of within them, like we did during our time on Earth, when we were praying and helping to elevate the peace of those on Earth.

Astrid: Beautiful, thank you.

Spirit: Thank you for your presence.

Unwanted Reconnections

Astrid: Do You Have To Be With People You Don't Want To Be With In The Afterlife?

Spirit: No, unless you go to hell!

Astrid: Hi. Who are you and what's your name?

Spirit: I'm George, and my name is George.

Astrid: Hello, George. Thank you for being here. How fascinating you completely identify yourself with your name.

George: I am proud of who I am, and the name fits me well.

Astrid: So, George, since you stepped in, what's your answer to the question?

George: I already answered, but since you'd enjoy further development, let me tell you my story; I was burned. To death. (a lengthy pause follows)

Astrid: So you were angry? You hated those who burned you? You went to hell and came back? You had someone who died who came to see you and you previously hated that person? (He's being non-verbal right now, if you hadn't guessed.)

George: Well, it's a difficult situation when you are young. You trust, you have faith, and then you are killed. But you still have compassion toward them because somehow you understand.

Astrid: That's what I call seeing people you don't want to see.

George: When I passed, I saw them all behind the walls of my tunnel. How they were—their faces, their anger, their craziness. I didn't want to see them but I did.

Astrid: Why do you think that was?

George: I believe it was to show my soul that I was leaving it all behind, that they couldn't hurt me anymore. I was here and they were there. My passing felt much lighter for it.

Astrid: Oh great! Thank you. Would you like to add anything? Like why did you say, "Unless you're in hell"?

George: Souls coming back from hell have told me they saw everyone they didn't want to see there. Makes sense if you ask me.

Astrid: Have they—or yourself—seen any of them since then?

George: Yes, in fact I realized they were all souls I shared blueprints or threads with. Some have come back here, others not yet. Others have moved on.

Astrid: Even the really bad ones?

George: Yes. Great souls take on the worst.

Astrid: They should know better.

George: They usually do! (Laughter)

Is Heaven a Copout?

Astrid: It seems so easy to say anything and everything is possible; to imagine all these possibilities; to dump them all on alignment-based connections; and to call it a day. Who really knows if it's not just our ultimate imagination or some really twisted video game we are all a part of? Maybe Earth is just a piece of hash in a bong! And maybe I'm just talking to myself all day long. And now I don't even want to know what is said next because it's all in my head anyway.

So let's say our world is an intricate, unconscious bunch of matter and energy that connects, creates, forms, and identifies but with no real higher or super intelligence behind it other than the one we experience. Just for the sake of it, we accept beings from other worlds and dimensions with superior or inferior knowledge. So we are born, and like a plant we grow, we die or get chopped off, and nothing other than the roots or seeding can bring something that resembles us back. That's it. No afterlife, no heaven, no hell. A bunch of ashes. What do you, oh infinitely intelligent one, have to say about that?

Spirit: It is as you wish. Just be careful what you wish for!

Astrid: Today I asked a similar question; I asked about change and how we could cut emotions off. I wanted to know how it was, that we could drastically change our attitudes and live a completely different reality, whilst in the same circumstances. I noticed I reacted very differently to my son today compared to a time when I had been less tolerant and I wondered if this change in me had anything to do with practice.

Spirit: Practicing to repeat a new experience is always helpful. Having faith in its reality is even more helpful. The desire to align to the best you can be is the most helpful. But remember, it all stems from the fact that you are already great and that recognizing this and experiencing it consciously and willingly makes it be.

Astrid: So the practice of believing in heaven makes it real?

Spirit: Heaven is real to those who believe it. Those who act upon their belief experience heaven. Souls have made it a reality through the practiced experience of their belief.

Astrid: Are there souls in the afterlife that live without a heaven?

Spirit: Absolutely.

Astrid: I thought souls deceased realigned with their higher, greater selves. I thought that higher and greater selves were filled with love. I thought that the space of unconditional love is what heaven is all about. How can a deceased soul having retrieved itself to its higher self deny heaven?

Spirit: Greater selves also have the choice to be, to express themselves and to think as they choose. For some, heaven simply does not exist in their state of consciousness. It does not mean that they are without love, or that unconditional love does not exist. It simply means that their chosen mode of apparatus is not aligned with such thoughts or experiences. Certain souls also choose to seek the absence of it and how that may fit into the awareness of self. Heaven is not a given, it is chosen.

Do Souls Ever Just Die?

Astrid: Do souls ever just die? I mean like completely just go away?

Spirit: No, they never do. Souls are make-ups. They are not entities. The real entity is the spirit. The soul brings the spirit to experience itself in relationship with its environment and its desires.

Astrid: So when you say souls in the afterlife, what are we talking about?

Spirit: About the experienced identity you wish to talk about.

Astrid: Earlier, I was given the analogy of Russian dolls to explain what a soul may be and how a soul continues to be in the afterlife. You are telling me that this identification is a make-up and that the real entity is spirit. Could you please explain the notion of spirit?

Spirit: Think of spirit as a thought form. It is not condensed into matter. It does not exist as matter. It is thought. It is singular and multiple at the same time. It is active and stagnant at the same time. It is shared and unique at the same time. Spirit is one and many at the same time. Spirit consciousness is thought that recognizes itself as it is in the way it does.

Let's say that one day, all that is became aware of what it was. Thought gave birth to the notion of being. Thought produced the idea that it, Spirit, was something. Spirit gave itself form. Let's say spirit saw itself as a huge all-encompassing sun. This huge sun, that represents all that is, then decided to see what it was not. Spirit extended its consciousness outside of itself. The rays of the sun represent spirit consciousness striving to seek what is outside of itself. Each ray of sun reaches outside of the sun to explore what it may not be or yet have. Spirit extends itself through the rays of the sun, never being detached from all that is, yet exploring what it's consciousness does not hold in its experience of self. Spirit flows through everything, always being a part of everything but not always consciously experiencing itself as everything. Spirit is the thought consciousness that identifies itself within all that is, that it is.

Astrid: So spirit never dies. Why then don't souls die?

Spirit: Souls cannot die because souls represent the self within spirit. Take the Russian doll idea. The smallest may be a soul as a human. The bigger one may be the soul's higher self. The greater one may be the soul that holds all souls. Souls are the expression of spirit in life. Souls are the identification of spirit consciousness. Just as spirit never dies, the soul spirit chooses to embody cannot die too.

Back from Hell

Spirit: I was in hell. I was an angry black man having come back from slavery in my previous life. The minute I got triggered about it in the next life, when I came back as a black man, I was very, very angry and led a life of anger and frustration. However, my blueprint did not allow me to change my conditions without peace of heart, and I came in with poor conditions to help motivate me to make a change, including a change of heart. From the life of slavery to the life of an angry young man, the transition was short and I held a lot of blame on God for letting me go through so much without more help. I refused to go to the light because I wanted to continue the fight, and I found myself in hell.

Everyone around me was angry, and anger just built over and over again. I witnessed tortures and killed more for it, becoming stronger and more resilient in the process. But the compassion wasn't there. I was frustrated at myself and everyone else, times a thousand, and the more I got frustrated, the more frustrations came. There was no moment of peace. Where my fears went, I went. Where my anger went I was already there.

I was starting to get used to it and found satisfaction in what I did.

Astrid: How did you get out?

Spirit: I met a soul who said he recognized me as his father. Of course everyone lies there, so I didn't believe him, and I actually killed him a few times over in hell. After the last time, he didn't come back for a long, long time. But since that meeting, I started having dreams, and I was dreaming he had been my boy. This lasted quite a while without me changing ways, but these dreams became my friends, and I would take them with me and start talking to them as if they were real. The boy in my dreams and I eventually started discussions on strategy and what would make the best sense in my hellish way of life. One day the boy came back. The boy had grown up angry, just like me, and was sitting right beside me. Up until then, the dreams had just been like flashes and no emotions were shared, just a presence and the same feelings of anger and more anger.

Then one day, I had another dream that changed everything. The boy was just a baby and I had hit him hard to stop him from crying. I felt a feeling, and although I didn't quite understand it, it hit hard inside me. What had I seen to make me feel? I would only remember later; I saw the look of fear in the boy's eyes. I woke up disturbed because all I could think was, why wasn't he angry? This dream repeated over and over, and the more I saw it, the more I tried to figure it out. At last, the idea of love came to me. I hadn't loved for eons. I hadn't cared to love. Nobody had loved me. I had been an orphan. I had been a slave. I had been whipped to shape me up, and I had done just the same to my son because all there was in life was the anger and the fight. A strong man is a man who doesn't give up to pain but turns it around to give a lesson. This was all I knew, all I cared about. It was all I was out to prove.

The dreams changed me. I took a closer look at possible reasons for my son's fear. Ideas of kind parents came to me. People around me started acting weird, and I became a target. But I held onto my dreams, and that's how I got out.

Astrid: What did you experience next?

Spirit: It was progressive. I spent a long time figuring out that what was in me was reflected outside me. So I started forcing myself to think differently. I died several times over and over again, coming back to the same state and getting ripped apart. But the deaths were not like when you die after living on Earth. You don't forget. You just come back as you were before you died. You never really die; you have the impression of death because you get killed or you kill yourself, but it doesn't change who you are. As I started to have more light in my soul, I found myself with the choice of thought, the choice of alignment, and then the choice of action. Desperation sets in and helps set you free. Anger turned to desperation is already a call for help, and the light of desperation takes over the darkness of the anger.

Astrid: What about hope?

Spirit: I believe hope never leaves you. It's just what you do with it that matters. I was not one to hope. To me, everything was the way it was, and I couldn't change it. I could only live with it and do it better. My anger fueled my way of life. When desperation set in, I didn't have as much anger. I was fighting for my life and was figuring out what that meant. Hope, or the realization of hope, only came later.

Astrid: Were you helped?

Spirit: Everyone was helping everyone else, even in hell. They acted, and we acted like we didn't, but we were reflecting each other and couldn't see it. When my perspective started changing, I started seeing more help, and eventually, I saw my guardian angel.

Astrid: Your son?

Spirit: Yes, my son. He never left me. He was there with me all along. We retrieved ourselves from hell together, with the power of the light to guide us.

Astrid: What would you say to people who fear hell?

Spirit: If you fear it, look away and do otherwise. Do better for yourself. Pain is not the only way of living. It's an interesting aspect to visit, but you don't have to be in it forever. Also, there is always help. There will always be a dream for you to align to. There will always be a soul to watch out for you. No matter how many times you die, or relive the same thing over and over, the mere fact that you still believe you are alive is a testimony to the light you have in you.

Loss of Senses

Astrid: When Do We Completely Lose Our Senses?

Spirit: It is very clear working and talking to spirits that life is really about a spiritual journey. Unfulfilled wishes and desires are only so because the goal was no match to the soul's intent for growth. You notice others around you having the material things you want while you do not. This is because you, as a soul, have asked to progress spiritually first.

What is first attached to the material leaves. Physical attachments like the body and the brain separate from the soul's experience first. Patterns of thought, just like habits of the body, leave instantly. This is when the soul realizes how much of a soul it has been throughout its life. For many, bliss takes over. It is like going through the first suction of a mother's milk backward. Our souls remember where home is. They are always connected to home, and home is where bliss is!

The return takes you through your processes, letting go of the most mechanistic as the soul liberates itself to be its truest self. However, as noted above, the life journey is first the soul's journey. If the soul is not satisfied, it will fight and deny itself access home before finishing what it sought out to accomplish. The return includes status on the soul's goals and its blueprint programming, and the allowance it gives itself to go home. It is not the decision of the dead brain. It is the soul's decision. What people forget is that those who were close to their soul's mission, in thought and action, are the souls who, in the afterlife, finish anything they hadn't before passing on. This is true to all soul levels and states of being.

The first encouragement we give you is, in the present, align more in joy and faith with what you call your higher consciousness, self, or mind. Live your highest self through checking your thoughts and choosing which ones you really want to belong within you. Take action with respect to this best self.

The timing of letting go has everything to do with the mind that is beyond that which is no longer physically linked. Everything cellular disconnects, but every memory is kept intact. The soul may retrieve these memories in its afterlife journey at will, or be triggered by them, in which case change is claimed. When change is claimed is when the soul reconsiders itself in the moment. This moment may be tied to the immediate past life, and this is when, for example, you will see ghosts of past loved ones. Or it may be claimed as a progression within the journey through the afterlife. In which case the soul may become a student there, or wish to be reborn for further growth within those earthly alignments.

Souls in the afterlife may portray behaviors they were recognized for in their previous life. These attachments are willed. As much in hell as in heaven, it is first the will of the soul that determines its fate. Very few humans who pass from life on Earth through death are capable of the control of their awareness in passing. For that to be, the soul and the mind have to be in sync with will and purpose to make it through the transition cognitively speaking. Emotional attachments are none other than electromagnetically charged connections of thought running through the energetic field of a being. These are absolutely everywhere. It is easy for a departed soul to continue to portray the human traits it once had. All it needs to do is align in vibration with these traits. In the same way, it is as easy to recall the vibrational alignments of a deceased loved one through these personality traits, but it does not mean the soul hasn't moved on. It may or it may not have.

To inspire them to greater vibrations is what prayer is all about, and this is our second encouragement to you: send uplifting intentions to the spirits you connect with. This will not only lift yours but theirs. At the time of death, the spirit lifts. The moment of death is never slow. The body may slowly shut down, but the spirit lifts off quickly. In one breath it leaves the body forever. The cognition may linger. This is what allows for the souls to visit their loved ones before they pass on, or to deal with issues they want resolved before they allow for themselves, as souls, to move on. The spirit is the drive of the soul's essence to be. The soul is the actual source of form that identifies itself in the experience of what the spirit ignites. You can consider the spirit as the light in the ray of sun, and the soul is the actual ray, or any part it identifies with in the experience.

In regards to loosing one's senses, the sensations a soul has had in life leave as soon as the soul's journey within them is over, including what the soul may choose to continue to experience in the afterlife. Bottom line is, you leave when you are done with what you had and you choose to have otherwise. Our last encouragement to you is to truly focus on what you would enjoy better. In so doing, you will ignite those soul alignments to joy and bliss that are within you. You will truly gain a greater perspective and a most fabulous sensation of who you are as a soul. You will better understand the choices of personality and actions you have given yourself. Finally, you will make things better for yourself and others as you know what you desire more of within your greater self.

Fun in Heaven

Astrid: What Do Souls Do In Heaven For Fun? But before you answer that question, I feel I need an answer to this one first: Is there excitement, joy, and fun in heaven, and if so, why not with its opposite?

Spirit: An opposite feeling doesn't have to be experienced. Oppositions are not everywhere. We are in a place of no oppositions. Only love and joy.

Astrid: Okay, so how do you evaluate fun?

Spirit: We evaluate it by the intensity of the expected experience. In heaven, some things are just a given. You do not need to toil for food. You don't even have to breathe. But everything is accessible. Fun becomes a momentum, and in an inkling of a thought, the soul may find the experience of it. When you get the hang of it, it's really fun!

Astrid: So, back to my first question; what do souls do in heaven to have fun. What does that look like, feel like, sound like to you?

Spirit: It is bliss. It is pure enjoyment. It is more than one could ever expect. It is spontaneous. Fun in heaven is part of the experience in heaven. Joy, fun, laughter, smiles;

all are present in the bliss souls in heaven live. When you are in bliss, you are in joy, you have fun, you laugh, you smile, you live a blissful experience all around.

Astrid: And how did you get there? I mean, it sounds so much further than what some of us here can ever expect.

Spirit: Expectation is the knowingness and the drive to fulfill a desire. You decide what to expect. For that, you have tentacles of sorts: alignments, connections, feedback, outlook. Everyone uses these tentacles for their soul purpose. One of the ways we purposefully use ours is to seek out enjoyment. This search takes us into a multitude of timelines, situations, and movements to find and experience it, sometimes just as observers, or students, other times as direct participants, entertainers in the act. We do enjoy laughing at ourselves and each other. On our level there is no need for tears of sadness in order to have tears of joy.

We encourage you to seek joyful sensations in your life. They may seem riddled with moments of fear or other negative sensations, and you very well may question the balance between them in your experience, but we guarantee that if you put your mind toward joy, you will have more of it.

Astrid: Could you give us some examples of moments of joy in heaven?

Spirit: Study groups in the afterlife enjoy exploring through spirit worlds we, as souls, have never experienced.

Some souls are eager to learn about Earth before they go there. Their spirit will dwell momentarily in the energetic field of an entity on Earth. For instance, many use nature, plants, flowers, and trees to learn the sense of nature, including touch, smell, and taste. It is so fun to project one's self into your scenery. It is hilarious seeing ourselves projected with long noses to smell, or huge ears to hear. Spirits may swing on branches or sway in fields of wheat. They may experience the joy of the oceans with the dolphins or being amongst the multitude of stars upon which wishes are cast. Study groups can be really fun!

Astrid: So souls use their spirit to experience things? That sounds backward.

Spirit: Consider the spirit the flow and the soul an element of the flow.

Astrid: Wow, so souls are really tiny!

Spirit: (Laughing) Without them, what else may be? Within the flow of spirit lies all its elements of its experience. It's like a huge web in a multitude of dimensions. Consciousness runs through it like electricity, wired here and there and everywhere. Where there is consciousness there is identification, which may take many forms, or not. These constitute the worlds you know, the many we speak of, and the many more we have not yet experienced. Within this conscious expression lies the place of a soul. Spirit consciousness aligns, gives itself a form to experience itself in, conscious of its temporal identity and brings life to that which it seeks, self-identified. That is one form of a soul as you know it.

Astrid: What does that mean?

Spirit: It means there are other forms of souls. Those souls who do not give themselves a form, for example, but who are given one, or none.

Astrid: Subjected souls?

Spirit: Exactly.

Astrid: Wow, so you can take a soul and just plant it somewhere else.

Spirit: Only certain ones. Souls may refuse to be subjected. It is the force of spirit and the soul's free will that prevails.

Astrid: Do these subjected souls exist in heaven, and if so, how do they have fun?

Spirit: Yes they do. Everything and anything is possible, as you say so well. Subjected souls find fun in being so and there are many ways they express their enjoyment. Fun lightens the load, and heavenly souls make a point of seeking lighter states of being through joy.

Animals in Heaven

Astrid: Do animals go to heaven?

Spirit: Oh, yes, animals have their heaven too. It's like this. Imagine each vibrational alignment type having their own heaven, but these heavens connect, and beings from one can go to visit beings from another. That's exactly how it is with our pets. They have their own stream of life and we can, as souls in the afterlife, reconnect with them at ease. So you may visit the animal heaven, in particular where your pets roam freely, and they may step into your experience in the afterlife and be present with you there.

Astrid: What about pets that have the attitude of men or woman? They seem to be people. Do they go to the animal kingdom or the people's heaven?

Spirit: (Laughing) There is no such thing. It's all about the level of vibration. Kingdoms are spaces where kinship happens, for multiple reasons. As it is in heaven. Many forms exist and coexist. Just like on Earth. Some souls come in as pets having previously lived the life of a human. There is no level in form in the way you were taught. There is only level of vibration. Eventually, vibration is such that form is meaningless within it. Or, to put it another way, it has no purpose to be.

Astrid: Okay, back to our animals. When a squirrel is hit on the road, for example, where does it go?

Spirit: Souls that decide to live the life of an animal are very restricted. Their soul purpose is to have that experience, which is one much more of equilibrium than it is of driven intent. Animals on Earth balance the ecosystem they are part of. Their duty is ingrained in them. At the smallest level, all they know coming in is to do a job. That's the prerequisite. No more, no less. Pets bridge the gap for humans to associate themselves with the souls of those who chose such tasks. The hit squirrel will go through the process of death without many of the attachments a human soul will—just conscious of its experience and accomplishments.

Astrid: Does that mean we don't find animals in hell?

Spirit: Not many! Remember, the form is nothing but a means of identification related to what attachments the soul has in the moment. The souls in hell who chose to better themselves through the skin of an animal, but didn't, will go back to hell. Souls in hell often choose animal or insect skins in rebirth to help them retrieve their soulfulness.

Astrid: So souls in hell have a chance to redeem themselves through critters and lions?

Spirit: Yes, as their souls are still attached with such intentions as self-worth. It is easier for their spirit to encompass the form of a mouse than a human whose relationships are more primary to its evolution.

Astrid: In the afterlife, given we are good souls and are in heaven, where and how do we meet our pets?

Spirit: In the same way you would any other soul you want to reach out to. You vibrate the love that you share, and you intend upon a visit or encounter. And so it is.

Astrid: Do pets meet us human souls when we die?

Spirit: Oh, absolutely! Their spirit is ever-present to those who loved them. They will stick around and be made known. A human with a pet that crossed over will feel, hear, smell, or even see the pet's spirit just like they would a father or daughter who passed away.

Astrid: Not everyone sees them. What do you suggest to people who want to reconnect but cannot?

Spirit: Trust that the love you feel transcends all time and space. Trust that they are all in a better place for themselves and for the betterment of all. Trust that when you call out to them, through your thoughts of endearment, they hear and respond. Trust and expect. Keep an open mind. Language is only universal through the open mind and loving heart. Only then will the signs make sense. Allow for the serendipity, the surprising coincidence that connects you. These are moments of connections.

Ways to Reconnect

Spirit: I lost my mom in life when I was five. I died when I was twenty-five. While I was alive, I felt my mom's presence, but there was always doubt in my mind if this was true. She was the first one to greet me on the other side.

She explained the threads that kept us connected and that the notion of love was more of a state of being than an emotional asset. In each state of love there were connecting threads to all the souls everywhere, and like freeways, this love could help us travel to those we wanted to be with.

Astrid: Why do you think you had trouble believing your mother was still talking to you?

Spirit: I wanted to believe she was still there. I wanted to believe the voices I heard were real. I think it has to do with our makeup as humans and what we are told to believe.

Souls here tell of lives past, where communicating with us in the afterlife is part of life. They had no problem relating to their ancestors and deceased friends. They did not question their experiences. I was not brought up that way in my past life, although now I understand why. But for those that deny, ignore, or doubt their connections to their loved ones, the passing of someone can be painful for a long time.

Astrid: What happens to the ignored souls who try to communicate with us?

Spirit: Usually they are not alone when they communicate. There is an entire section here dedicated to making the reconnection easier on both sides. Souls learn how to modulate their vibrations to connect with the density of thought on Earth. They are taught what works best according to the energetic alignments of those on the other side and how best to communicate their loving support. When a person ignores the messages, they still receive the vibrational alignment of love from us here because we use the same threads of love with which the person resonates. It is then up to them to believe or not the experience they have. Many times people do not respond. They think they are mourning when in fact they are receiving love. They think they have no connection when in fact the connection is made stronger.

Souls here do not doubt. They do not have feelings like that of the human body. They do not have personalities and attitudes like they do when they are alive. Their differences are first and foremost based on their vibrational alignments. Souls group here according to what they vibrate as a soul. Our families are all of us. We recognize who we spent time with not by what they look like but by what they vibrate. It's a knowingness of who's who without anyone being any one in particular. My mother is also the soul who has birthed many others present here, who have birthed and died before me. She is not just my mother but the soul energy who has expanded through many others, including myself. When we get together, it's like magnifying the light and love we both share. At a higher level of consciousness, we are together as one greater soul existence. But for now, we appreciate the difference and our experience of it together. This is why souls do not take it badly when those they seek to help through reconnection ignore them. They, we, know we are still connected and that our support, even if not consciously acknowledged in life, is still very much present.

Astrid: How do you help those who mourn their loss?

Spirit: Once we have figured out what works best for them, we just apply the principles of love. We too have spaces of directed intention, prayer temples, or places of worship, if you will. These are specifically designed to hold the vibrational space for reconnection. They are like energy centers where driven intention can be purposefully directed to the most minute element in all of time and space the vibration matches. It's like a power circle of love that can drive our intentions out into the universe.

There are also spaces where we can actually observe what is going on with people. These are not given to everyone because of the risks of disengaging from your current vibrational alignment. If the soul isn't strong enough to maintain its own alignments while connected to others, it will not venture to reconnect in this way. Only the strongest can observe the emotional state of those on Earth without the help of guides.

Astrid: How is life on the other side now?

Spirit: Life is good! Everyone is good. Everyone is well. I am remembering that I have always been here and that there has always been a part of me here. Just like beyond where I am now, there I am too, with perhaps a wider range of existence and less focus on a specific place of experience. For now, I enjoy the space I am in. I have my past mother, my past brother, and many friends and family members from previous lives. It is paradisiacal in the sense that it resembles life on Earth with beautiful landscapes, happy moments of play, exploration, and reunification. I have chosen to live simply with my favorite animal friends who come and go between their dimension and ours. When I desire to see children at play, I think of them with love and they appear in front of me as if I was on the sides of a playing field. I can then interact or not. Here I am able to connect with my daughter I left behind, as her soul presence is very much alive here. She sees me in her dreams and sometimes hears me too. She will respond to me.

Astrid: What happens if she has negative thoughts or feelings toward you?

Spirit: Her soul vibration weakens here as it concentrates on the point of focus she gives herself. It weakens our distant communication abilities and tugs on my soul's alignments too as we share the same alignments. I still have work to do to help her dissipate the emotional walls of thought conditions, but we are together and love each other dearly.

Timing

Astrid: How long does it take for a soul to be able to send messages to their loved ones? How is that done?

Spirit: Not long at all. First the departing soul has the ability to visit their loved ones in a very strong manner, during what you know as the three days after death. Many of you are visited during your sleep or meditation time as it is easy for the departing soul to connect in love without your mental obstacles getting in the way.

Once the passing is over (and this may take much less than your three day awareness), the departed soul finds itself in a new space, with new vibrational alignments, and these may not be conducive to connections with those left behind. The question is, is the grieving person able to tune into the departed soul's new level of vibration? For those who go to the lighter realms, such as those connected to your religious or other great mentors, the soul will find it easy to reach out to those on Earth who ask for their presence. They align with your soul at a greater level and it is easy, through this union up above to whisper through your self here on Earth. For souls staying in closer or lower vibrational levels to consciousness on

Earth, they may also easily be heard, seen, or felt as their energies connect to what you are familiar with. In their case, however, their energies may be too disconnected to come through to you. The lost ones will follow and communicate with those living who match their vibration the best.

The grieving person has trouble disengaging from the emotional body vibrations and alignments, and this may take time to do. From the perspective of the departing soul, they will welcome your call and respond when they are ready to realign with the vibrations you offer in the moment of communication. The better your inner peace, the greater clarity you will have and the better and longer the communication. In any regard, it is the focused attention of thought vibrations that latch onto your consciousness while your emotional body and soul connections and recognition tells you who is there. For you to be better aware, you may listen to your body and thoughts by allowing thoughts to pass by while paying attention to any inner or outer physical reaction. This will help you determine who or what is coming to you and how you feel about it.

On Earth some rejoice while other shed tears of sadness. The rejoicing is the inspiration to the departing soul to seek its heights. The sadness, unfortunately, may hold souls down and make their passing longer. The notion to let rest a departing soul is a good idea. It is a good time for those grieving to rest their thoughts too and realign with their soul essence. In doing so, the reconnection may be immediate. Souls departed have absolutely no control over the living soul, unless it is part of the agreement. But even then, the higher self is always on the watch out to allow free will of spirit to be, including as an element of the soul, wherever it may be. The free will of all soul is what ultimately defines its connections and the time it takes to do so.

Helping to Transition

Astrid: How Can People Help The Transition Of A Soul? (This is such a loaded question; I want to keep it to channeling. Or make another book out of it! What I personally would enjoy is an angelic answer as they are always so profound to the many who hear) How can people help the transition of a soul?

Spirit: Through love.

Astrid: (I laugh at myself at the answer from spirit. Serves me right!)

Spirit: Love conquers all. Love is the source of being. Love the best way you can, always with respect to your soul self, and always for the betterment of all. Then souls find their way to where their desires are met and their soul families unite.

Astrid: What if, in life, we don't really care what happens to certain souls? What if we don't want to give them light?

Spirit: A prayer to your problem-solving spirit guide with belief, faith, and expectation suffices. (Saint Michael is very efficient with me.) If you fear alignment to the soul or spirit, you can acknowledge yourself as a cub in a dark, scary forest, and help you ask for will be given through the hearing spirit of your soul parents. Just as you in the dark forest, departed souls always have the choice to remain in the dark, or to go forth into the light. This is ultimately their choice, but it is not the person departed you know who is responsible for this choice. It is the soul of this person, and this soul is much greater than you think. It is very true that spirit delves in many places at the same time, in many times at once—the rays of the sun going in multiple directions with multiple intensities from its source self. This is true. So do you. Souls desire to lift off, to explore, experience, self-realize in so many ways and forms. So when the soul gets stuck, it is natural for it to call out. The call is always answered. You may hear it, or a stranger may hear it in this realm or another. Then the soul has the choice and free will. Love permeates all. Use that to uplift any soul, spirit, or stone.

Short Spontaneous
Responses from Spirit

Astrid: Does the Grimm Reaper exist?

Spirit: Yes, in many forms. At the time of death, there is always the presence of a helping soul and this soul may take the form of what you know as the Grimm Reaper.

Astrid: Is baptism necessary to go to heaven when you die?

Spirit: No. Although there is great uplifting with the power of mass intent.

Astrid: What happens to atheists?

Spirit: The name drops. The meaning changes. The journey continues.

Astrid: Lost souls—why are they stuck? Can they get out?

Spirit: Many for the same reasons you are here. Anyone can get out of being "a two." Becoming a "greater one" is the surest way to go.

Astrid: When do we completely lose our senses?

Spirit: Never. Numbing them or cutting them off doesn't help them disappear either. Sensorial systems are part of the entire makeup of existence. Stretch your senses, dig deeper to gain more knowledge of them, and practice all your senses to vibrate to the sensations that feel the best to you.

Astrid: Time is different there. Do they have routines? What is a typical day there?

Spirit: It depends where you are. Where your consciousness gets stuck, if you will. For some, it flies off to heaven where they can have the routine of their dreams. Others stick around your dimension and may even have the same routine as they just had on Earth. But have no fear. They may seem many to you, but it is truly just many times a residual energetic trap of consciousness, which will transform to its own accord for the greater one it comes from.

Astrid: What do you do with religious beliefs?

Spirit: Religious beliefs, just like laws, are based on a philosophy of thought applied to action. Choose what you wish to believe and experience the journey with a good heart, mind, mouth, and hand. Value the words of wisdom that touch you to be better. Have faith in yourself. Be smart, be curious, question, make better. Follow your purpose.

Astrid: Do souls meet God?

Spirit: Oh, many do. I love the way God's image changes to the liking of this soul or that. Determine what you consider God and you may one day meet its representation in the light of the afterlife.

Astrid: What do you do when your child sees spirit all the time?

Spirit: (Laughing) Me, I would do nothing! If you were to build something with your child, would you build a tower of fear or a tower of joy? Now sit and think before you go answer your child.

Astrid: How do they decide how much the human is allowed to know about his or her Akashic records?

Spirit: They that you speak of is a term subjective to the many that may only be one. The higher soul always decides what it may retrieve in knowledge to further its quest.

Astrid: Why do some humans get to see more of the Akashic records than others?

Spirit: Because they are better aligned to them. Purpose, blueprint, intent, and free will of the soul are your best bets to enter the records room.

Astrid: Why are we so tied to our emotional body?

Spirit: You are tied with purpose to your emotional bodies.

Astrid: Why would we rather laugh than be there crying then?

Spirit: Liberation. You are liberating the ties of your emotional body to that which the soul desires to change. It is very liberating to the soul to enlighten the emotional body. And the physical body finds great strength in it too.

Astrid: Can we predict a happy ending?

Spirit: You think of time as a challenge, yet every time you have come back to Earth, it was for exactly that specific time. You come back, you continue to shape and form and change and shape and form again. You are always seeking happiness within it. Otherwise why do it?

The difference with this time is that you have given yourself greater awareness of yourself and of your powers of change and creation. This is a spectacular time! You have risen to the challenge and have changed much of yourself in a very short amount of time. Do more so consciously in seek of the happiness you dream of, and you will understand me better.

The Value of Souls

Astrid: I would like to add to these shared exchanges a point in value. In our world right now, there's a lot of weight given to the monetary, financial exchange in value and I wanted to know what spirit has to say about that.

Spirit: It's a game. Just like everything else. We enter a game of life to play it, just like we enter a game of Monopoly, chess or Mahjong. Exchanging with value has always been. Every soul finds value to its participation in life. Otherwise, why would it be?

Astrid: there have been quite a few that have killed themselves or others over it!

Spirit: Indeed a choice of action.

Astrid: In deed?

Spirit: Indeed!

Astrid: What is the value the soul gives itself that it never dies?

Spirit: That of love.

Astrid: So what if souls explore spaces where there is no love? Since everything and its opposite exist, what happens then?

Spirit: It is up to the soul to choose how to respond. A soul always knows deep down that it comes from love, otherwise, why would it be?

Astrid: How about simply to be nasty or indifferent. Is a soul capable of being without love in itself?

Spirit: No, love, is at the core of all that is.

Astrid: So you bring value down to love?

Spirit: Expressed love is not always lovey-dove, as you'd say. A desire can clash with another ones intent and sparks may fly. Those who love what they do, what they create, achieve or express, always win. They win for themselves and it ripples out to others. The financial aspects of achievements play out through the links the soul has to the many worlds of finances. How does a soul relate to cash, riches, poverty, markets and economics? Where does a soul place itself as part of the game? What beliefs does the soul come in with and which ones does it choose to experience?

Astrid: The same questions can be geared toward relationships, in a way.

Spirit: Exactly.

Astrid: How do you value your soul self?

Spirit: I have my ups and downs like you. I appreciate the rest here, having gone through a period of stretch, of which I am proud of, no less. I sometimes wish I had things that do not come immediately. It's not always the case, and you and I know sometimes we need to just take it as it is because there's a reason, and we'll figure it out.

Astrid: Wow. It doesn't seem like you are in blissful heaven.

Spirit: I think heaven is an ultimate we are always reaching for, and as long as we long for something different, we will always be seeking it! Just like the game of monetary value. Sometimes it is wise to stay still and appreciate what we have in the now. We can have bliss whilst being still.

Astrid: I want to point out how great it is to have a drive, to be excited about getting up every morning, and sometimes in the middle of the night to be doing the things you love, to aspire to make a difference and to know that rewards may come from it.

Spirit: Yes, that is when you thrive.

Astrid: So you are not thriving?

Spirit: I am at rest. I have thrived. I am happy and proud. Now I am in a period of rest and contemplation.

Astrid: And that's when one may gets newly inspired, right?

Spirit: For change, yes. Otherwise, you can live in love with a sense of completion and wonder and that's heavenly bliss in itself!

Astrid: What would you say to souls seeking monetary value?

Spirit: I would hope they seek to do well with it. In the end, it's all about what you do with what you have, for the love of yourself and others.

PART 3

Prayers and Exercises

*Prayer is of the asking. Exercising
is good practice to manifest.*

A Prayer to Say Goodbye

I, (your full name), ask to the highest

That the greatest love and light be bestowed upon the soul of (name your loved one),

As it rises to new heights.

I trust that we are always together beyond that which differentiates us,

And in our differences, we enjoy each other's loving presence as needed.

I ask that in our sorrows and joys we may continue to share and exchange

So we may grow in greater experiences of love and joy together.

To you, dearest loved one,

I send you my love, knowing that in some way, you will receive it.

As I love you now, I wish you a fare and joyful way,

Hoping from the bottom of my heart that you may come to visit often.

So as you are now, and as we stand today,

Wishing for nothing less than for you to be by our sides and us at yours,

Go in peace, in love and light,
And know you are loved,
Now and forever,
Amen.

A Prayer of Peace

My dear and departed loved one, (name),
With whom I have had issues with,
From which my soul has grown,
Today I say to thee,
With as much love as my heart can muster,
And as much light my mind can take,
I am sorry,
I forgive,
I thank myself as I thank thee,
I love you as I love me.
(Feel free to add to any of the four statements above.
Feel free to do so as often as you like.)
Peace and happiness be with you now and forever.
Amen/and so be it.

A Prayer for Pets

As I write this, I prepare also for the death of my horse. I dedicate this prayer to his great spirit, thanking those of the equine heaven for helping him through it and being so grateful to my own guides for helping me and my family through it too.

Dear loved one,

As I embrace with love the memories we shared and those I was absent for,

In the presence of your most loving guides and friends,

And in the presence of mine,

We thank you for your love, for your presence and guidance in my life and in the life of all those you shared.

Your great spirit will always be with us, as it is already with the many that await you now.

I ask to them all to help you and guide you through an easy and happy transition,

As you depart from the body we know, to your Heaven where you may be free in form,

Where you may rejoice of the wonderful accomplishments you have done here with us and the many more to come.

Blessed spirit,

Rest from this world knowing you are at peace and forever loved.

Come and say hi to us anytime!

Hugs; I love you.

Amen/so it is/so be it.

A Prayer Of Faith

In this time of need I turn to my greatest loving self for help,
Desiring in mind, heart, and soul
That my heart finds comfort,
That peace fills my mind,
That my soul lives in joy.
May what has bothered my thoughts, heart, and soul be gone now,
As I turn to love and light for solace, enlightenment, and joy.
May this joy, light, and love engulf me now and guide me to better be,
With and through my heart, mind, and soul, as I am willing to be.
Amen, and so it is.

A Prayer for Soul Healing

As I experience the troubles of my life
And the difficulties I experience related to them,
I believe in my higher self and the unconditional love
I come from

As I strive to reach this loving consciousness, for
myself and others
I offer as much of it as I have, knowing that love
heals all

In so doing, I release the emotional negativity attached
to me
I give myself through it the love I need
And I rise myself to a more loving conscious state of
being.

What I have experienced may now bring change to
better be
In greater ways of my soul's self-expression.

Dying to Recycle

Throughout my life, I have been curious of death. I've wondered why? How? For what purpose do we bring ourselves through the process of dying? In my search, spirit has given me so many insights, coupled with exercises to better be.

One of these exercises includes the understanding of recycling. As we poop, we help the recycling process. As we die, we engage in the same process. Nature, earth, the planet have been nurtured by the recycling process for eons. I asked souls if our emotions are human baggage we also throw in the recycling process and they said yes, they are. Our emotions are vibrational elements of life created that are also rid of at the time of death. Like ashes, they lay down to rest whilst continuing to participate in the co-creation of tomorrow. Emotions just don't disappear. They too are recycled. In fact imprints of emotional energies may stay stagnant in places on Earth in such a way that animals, and even humans, can detect them.

Before departing and leaving our emotions as dust for others to deal with, this is what spirit (soul consciousness) recommends we do; take your current emotion and give it a name. Then give it a persona. Draw a circle on a piece of paper with two eyes, a mouth, eyebrows and ears and modulate this face to express the emotion you have. If you like it, keep it with you as a friend. If you do not like it, cross it out, flip the piece of paper and on the other side draw the face of the emotion you would rather have. This transmutes your initial emotion into one of greater quality that you may have as you see the transformation happening from one side of the page to the other. In all likelihood, this will bring a smile to your face and you may even start to draw happy faces every time you want to flip a negative emotion into a positive one.

I personally use the happy face over oil paintings I do when I don't like them. It's my way of sending them off with a smile to paint a better picture over them. This is how I recycle my paintings from unwanted to wanted ones. The old painting is dead, recycled to better serve and in the process, the original strokes of brush enhance the finished result.

We are not to feel ashamed of our emotions. They guide us to know the difference between what we enjoy and what we don't. But we don't need to hang on to them. They don't need to determine or be a part of our future. Allow for yourself to let the unwanted go and strive to focus on those you desire to experience more of.

Helping to Transition

Following are tips and tools to use to help a loved one better transition.

Say a Prayer

Anything you intend in love and light connects in love and light and enhances the experience in love and light. This is true as much for you, who is reaching in thought through love and light, as it is for the soul that is being reached. Prayers are of the asking as meditation is to the receiving. Ask and it shall be received, always. State your name as the one asking. This will put a stronghold on the connection that your thoughts and heart emit. It will act like a powerhouse, or like the spark when you turn the ignition key. The stronger the spark or drive, the more power is placed on the expected results. I always start my prayers for others like this; Dear God, my name is Astrid, Therese, Marie Cousin-Stromberg (my full name including my maiden name) and I pray that...The best way to pray is to simply ask. Ask that this or that shall be done, through the love and light you send out with your conscious intent and answered by the most wonderful love and light consciousness you can imagine. When asking, allow yourself to be in the most peaceful and loving inner place so nothing gets in the way of your intention in your field of energy. Then let it go. Ask and know it is received, immediately. Know that when the time is right, the signal of an answer will be made apparent to you. And if you doubt your signs, ask they may be made clearer. Open a dialogue of communication between yourself here and your other many great selves elsewhere.

Light a Candle

Candles are great connectors of thought and light in love. Upon lighting them, you may enhance the magnetic power of your thought by inviting spirit guides to align. Lighting a candle helps lift the spirit of the departed soul as it connects your prayer or intention to the loving guidance of those on the other side. You may use color-coding to link the frequencies of the color to your wishes. For example, orange is a color widely related to children, happiness and joy. Light an orange candle for a transitioning child.

Play some Music

Music often reminds us of our loved ones. Songs will pop up, a tune, a melody, sometimes an edited version of a song may weirdly come to mind. These are sure signs of your angels and loved ones telling you how present they are and how much they support and care for you. In return, you too can help through music. Use positive melodies to uplift both your soul and that of the one departing.

Faith in Reconnection

How does one have faith that our departed loved ones are still around? How can we be sure we are reconnecting with them? The best way to approach this is to expect that your loved ones do their possible to let you know they are still around. Expect contact, expect a sign and don't doubt. If in doubt, allow for yourself to doubt your doubt! Doubt all you want, and do question your doubt. Question yourself. Question your beliefs. Question what you are taught, what you read, and what you see on TV. Do not question your experiences, how you feel in the moment, or what thoughts pass you by. These are factual life moments for you. These you can trust. Become the observer of your experience of life, of how signs come to you, of what meaning they bring.

Here is an exercise to test the reconnection of a past loved one to you; when you think of a loved one on the other side, ask yourself immediately what you feel and what part of the body is being triggered in you. Where in your body do you feel a connection? Is your eyelid fluttering? Are your ears ringing? Did you just get goose bumps? Are you suddenly warmer or colder? Take a mental note of your physical reaction and see if this same reaction takes place the next time you connect with the soul. When signals are repeated, you become more assured of their source.

After noticing physical triggers, take head of your other senses and what they inform you of. For instance, do you notice a specific scent around you? Have you got a different taste in your mouth? Do you hear voices in your mind? Do your eyes have difficulty focusing in the moment? Did you just catch a shadow with your peripheral vision? Take note of all the immediate differences in sensorial perception and see if they get repeated with future connections. At first, you may not notice anything at all. Have faith. Keep testing your ways to reconnect. Imagine you are building a new language with your sensorial perception, and use your five senses to do so. A flicker of light where there was none, a perfume passing you by, a word or song that pops in your head; all these may be signs from beyond. Repetition will validate communication.

Communicating with the Afterlife

We all want to be able to talk to our loved ones once they are gone. We don't have cell phones or social media connecting us to the afterlife, but we do have our minds and soul connections to communicate with. Following are 8 steps to make the communication better and clearer between both sides;

Step 1: Allow

Allow the idea of communication between yourself and your departed loved ones to be possible.

Allow yourself to at least test things out. Allow for glimpses, flashes, weird noises, or familiar scents to be a sign. Allow for the fantastic to be possible in your life and consider that your loved one is sending you signals you can relate to.

Step 2: Connect

Thinking of a loved one connects. Whispering thoughts to a loved one connects. Holding an object dear to a loved one connects. Alignments connect. Know that the second you think, you connect. The second you feel, you connect. The second you smell, taste, sense, imagine, watch, hear, see … you connect. Yes, we are connected beings, for sure! Further those connections. Strengthen their ties through the vibrational alignments you have to your loved ones. For your departed ones, always choose the most uplifting and loving vibes. Both of your souls will unite in joy for as long as you want with joy in your heart. If there is only sadness, frustration, guilt, or anger, I suggest you step out of these alignments for yourself. Allow for the negative thought or feeling to pass you by. Send a prayer to the soul who is aligned with these thoughts, and ask the powers of love that be to help you. Consider yourself connecting every time you have a thought toward the departed and start a conversation as if they were right beside you.

Step 3: Accept

Accept your experience. Whatever you are thinking, feeling, and experiencing is your reality in the now. Experience is a factual moment in time for the one experiencing it. The change of heart and mind comes after the actual experience. Denying your experience is to deny the truth of what you sensed, which is contradictory to the mere fact we are sensorial beings. The faster you accept your experiences, the faster you can evaluate them and decide how to deal with them.

After much skepticism and doubt I finally accepted I had this gift to communicate with spirit. I was crying like a baby realizing that all this was true. Somehow, spirit gives me information that I could never have known otherwise. My brain feared judgment, my own self-criticism was the hardest to deal with. Who am I to say these things to people, to build up their hopes, or perhaps even scare them? But I had to accept the facts of my experience and the validations I continue to receive. Going into the unknown is scary. It challenges your thoughts, attitudes, and the worthiness of your actions. Accept yourself. Accept what you are capable of doing. Accept there is much more to all of this than you could ever imagine. Accept that worlds and dimensions are above and below and in all ways. Accept the fantastic, and the fantastic will show itself to you.

Step 4: Talk, Talk, Talk!

I used to yell at God. There was no doubt in my mind I had a direct channel to him (it was a him to me at the time). "How could you do this? How could you be that way? How could you allow us to experience this? You took my father away, a good man. I see others being bad; take them!" I'd yell. Yell all you want. And expect an answer. Answers always come. Immediately. In our frustration, we may not see it. We will deny it. Not good enough. Not strong enough. Not enough love back. Keep talking. State what you want more of. Want more love, better friends, greater rewards. Keep asking for an answer and pay attention to the signs that come.

Step 5: Pay Attention and Test

Pay attention to passing thoughts. Pay attention to a bird, a feather, a note with a big yes on it that you notice on your desk. Pay attention and request proof of communication. Test the signals. Test their repetitiveness and the circumstances they come under. Test the voice you hear in your mind, or the feeling you have walking through a door. Pay attention and test. Many times I have lapsed communication because I thought it wasn't good enough or strong enough. Who was I to say this was this person or that one? You will never be 100 percent sure, but when the same signs reappear, you become more certain.

Step 6: Have Faith in Certainty

When you communicate with spirit, what you want to do is always ask for the highest to come forth; the brightest light, the greatest love, the best insight, the best spirit guide. Wanting these matches your vibration to them and from there you can trust more easily. Good spirits will never ever say anything negative to you. They honor your feelings, they respect your experiences, and they allow you to have free will in all ways. This is a certainty you can be sure of.

Another certainty you can rely on is what you experience in the moment. Nothing can take that away from you. It is what it is. You had a feeling that was true. You had a thought; it happened. You had a flash; it flashed. No matter what your experience, it is what it is. What it becomes, what it can represent, what you do with it next becomes another experience. Patterns of experiences tell a story of alignments. Where you have a pattern, you have repetition, statistics in potentiality, predictability. Use patterns to communicate with your deceased loved ones to validate and strengthen the ties between you. Rituals, mantras, evening prayers ... these are all patterns with strong symbolic ties that help communicating between worlds. Patterns can help your faith in the certainty of what you experience.

When you do communicate, there's something inside you that knows this is for real. It might be for a split second, but it's there. Tell yourself that it was real. This will help your subconscious mind to trust the experience and to look out for more of the same. When spirit talks to me and I cannot write it down to remember, I tell myself, I got it. It's inside me, and whenever in the future I need this piece of information, it will be there, it will have seeded and worked in the direction my soul desires, and I will consciously or not work through and with what has been given to me to better be. It's like sending yourself a subliminal message to keep the great messages from spirit, from your higher self, from all those who want the best for you, inside your heart and mind so you can move on to better things or communicate in greater ways with your departed loved ones.

The first and last certainty you can tell yourself now is that you are love, you are great, and all those souls passed you wish to connect with now are and will always be with you. Unless you shut the door on them, and that's okay too!

Step 7: Choose to Be Together or Alone

Sometimes we really don't want spirit to see us. I have spirits in my bathroom, and I do not desire to have them see me there! The good news is, they don't see everything. Departed souls are able to check on us to know what's happening in our lives and to be present for certain events but it is more of a knowingness and an energetic connection, than an actual vision they have.

Our deceased parents know what we are doing. Our grandparents come in to visit as we sleep. Our angel guardians push us back to avoid an accident. We are definitely not alone. But sometimes the space feels crowded and you want to be alone. So say it and it shall be. You may feel a change in temperature in the room or even in your body telling you someone is around or leaving. Presence entails a shift in density, and density is something the body is very capable of sensing. Practice sensing the difference in energies around you, and you will quickly know when someone is there and, furthermore, if someone is coming. Then you can better invite or ask to leave.

Step 8: Talk the Way You Want to Be Talked To

Don't bother talking down to spirit. You'll only be inviting jokesters to play with your brain and twist it. Talk to spirit like you would enjoy being talked to. If you want a joke, ask for a joke. If you want some serious answer on an issue, ask for a serious answer on the issue. Be specific. Be respectful. Whatever vibe you offer is the vibe you expect connection with, so make it worth your while. And remember to always give thanks. Giving thanks is like allowing and accepting at the same time, knowing it is for your own good. Remember to refuse the negative. Negative entities only have value in the light of positive ones. Find your positive guides and helpers first before even thinking of going into the negative aspects of what you haven't experienced yet. There are places and spaces for everything. Align yourself with the best for your own betterment first, and then think about helping others elsewhere. And expect the same from spirit!

How to Deal with Guilt

Guilt is a sentiment, an emotional thought that can have repercussions on your physicality, just like all emotional thoughts. Having feelings of guilt is a curse and a blessing. It's a curse because it can get you nowhere, and it's a blessing because it opens up windows of self-understanding and self-love that you may not otherwise experience. When you have emotions of guilt, stop to consider them and then flip the feeling to bring out the emotion you would rather have. Following is an empowering exercise to help you deal with any negative emotions you have about yourself. I call it the Flip Game.

Take a piece of paper and split it into three columns. Title the first column Initial Thoughts. Under it, list any negative thoughts, sensations, and feelings that come to mind. Write as if you were doing a shopping list with bullet points. For example, my Initial Thoughts:

I feel so guilty it hurts.

I feel guilty I didn't say good-bye.

I feel guilty I yelled before she passed.

I feel guilty I wasn't there.

I feel guilty I didn't help enough.

List anything that comes to mind. Once you are done, title the second column I Would Rather. Use this second column to flip what you wrote in the first. In this column, opposite each bullet point from column one, write what you would rather have, think, do, feel, or believe. Only use positive wording. Turn around the negativity from column one in any way you can to write a positive thought you would rather have. It can be as silly as, "Right now, I would rather be smelling roses" or "I would rather be enjoying a cupcake". Anything you would rather be doing or having is better than the negativity experienced. The I Would Rather column will always reflect what's hidden inside you, and, as the goal of this exercise is to progress to a better emotional place, bringing out desires of well-being will do just that.

Title the third column My Blessings. In this column, you will write a blessing you have received related to the emotional situation you are exploring. For example, your blessing may be the memory of having eaten a cupcake with your deceased friend, and how much fun you had at the time. Your blessing may be the recognition of the love you have for the departed, or the time spent with them. In hardship there is always a blessing in disguise. Find your blessings and give thanks for having them. Subconsciously, what happens is that, with the third column, you reinforce the fact that the first statement may not be the only way to think. You tell your subconscious to produce better thinking patterns by doing this over and over. Soon you will not need your papers and lists. When a negative thought pops into your mind, you will immediately want to flip it into a positive one, and the negative thought will disappear. It doesn't mean the thought doesn't exist anymore. It doesn't mean you can't feel guilty anymore. The thoughts and feelings may still be there if you want them. But in practicing to flip negative emotions into positive ones, you will be happier and you will find greater love, joy and understanding for what happened and how it happened. Flip and see yourself move quickly toward greater self-love and compassion.

The hardest times to play the Flip Game are when we blow up with friends and family. In the moment it is not easy to be positive when things go badly. But even if you do not flip your thoughts in the moment, when you later recall these negative times, flip your thoughts into positive ones and this will diffuse their hold in the present.

Strengthening your Soul Self

These exercises are to have you understand how and for what purpose your personality—or what some of you call your ego—seems to get in the way, when in fact it is telling you what you want and how you'd enjoy it best. Read each sentence out loud and after each one, pause to receive insight before going to the next one. When you come across a question, write your answer on a piece of paper or on your tablet. Do not edit. Follow each exercise to the end and review.

In conclusion to each exercise, for greater results, write or think about what you learned from it regarding your soul self. Ask yourself how you can use this knowledge to bring out the best in you while still being you. Know that your subconscious mind has received all information and will naturally drive future thoughts and actions toward your goals. Only use positive wording. Enjoy the process!

To Like Attention

Where, when, and how do you like attention?

Being Right

When are you right? Give an example.

When do you feel happy about being right? Give an example.

Circle positive adjectives in both examples and highlight those in common.

Growing Up

Describe a significant moment of growth in your life.

Circle verbs.

Highlight adverbs.

Values and Etiquette

Write ten values and five principles of etiquette you appreciate.

Turn the paper over.

Sing a song out loud.

Write ten of your favorite animals (may include birds, mythological or ancient creatures, and critters).

Compare values and principles of etiquette with the animals, birds, etc.

Self-esteem and Self-worth

What is self-esteem to you?

How would that look?

What is self-worth to you?

How would that look?

Draw a picture that would have them both look their best to you, in the same frame.

Your Soul In Color

Have a piece of paper, a pen, and colored crayons ready. Take three deep breaths and invite your subconscious and conscious mind to align with your soul self.

Draw a dot in the center of your page.

Around that dot, draw a circle.

Around that one, draw another bigger circle.

Around that one, draw a third bigger circle.

Around that one do a fourth, and a fifth, and a sixth.

Name the dot Self.

Name the first circle Soul.

Name the second Body and Mind.

Name the third Chakra Body.

Name the fourth Emotional Body.

Name the fifth and sixth, respectively, the Aura and Ethereal Body.

Now imagine them all in their own dimension.

Let's consider the self first dimensional. The soul is second, the body and mind third, etc. How do you experience who you are within all these dimensions? From where you are in this third dimensional body and mind, how do you connect to your other dimensional experiences of self?

Take colored crayons and color in all the circles any way you want. Randomly pick your colors, or choose those that attract you or speak to you. Now sit back and let the colors speak to you. Jot down any thoughts that occur beside the colors and circles you have drawn. This tells how you are currently experiencing your multidimensional connections to yourself. Notice, in particular, how the first and second circles connect in colors together. This is how you currently connect to your soul self.

To decode your colors, and how they interact with each other, attribute them an animal, bird or insect, or link them to one of the five elements, earth, wind, fire, water, metal. For example, your inner circle of the soul may be a blue that reminds you of water. The second circle may be purple, to which you associate a bird. You may deduce from the water and the bird, that you are a free spirit in body and mind and that your soul is experienced mostly when the body and mind connect to the flows of inner self, or within your emotional body, if you will. Such a person would be well advised to work within the realms of creativity (free spirit), and to bring self-realization through lighter emotional experiences in life. The colors you intuitively choose always have a meaning attached. Associating them to symbols you relate to helps to uncover their meaning. Two circles with the same color may not ignite in you the same associated meaning. You might have the soul and the body and mind circles being pink, yet when focusing on the soul circle, the idea of a boat may appear whilst the second circle will be associated to a baby. You might be pregnant! Or you may interpret that as being on a soul journey in which you feel more like a child than a veteran in life. Allow your mind for interpretation to happen naturally, and you can do this exercise as many times as you want; each time you do the drawing, a new insight on yourself will appear.

Your Soul's Purpose

A soul's purpose is to experience change. It could be a change of heart, a change of mind, a change of form, a change of attitude or perspective, a change in the way you live, or even a change in the way you die. A soul always seeks to be a participant in change. As humans, we get confused. We think of goals and dreams as being our purpose, but when they don't happen, we ask ourselves why, or is it not meant to be? Wise men will tell you that time will tell. Time isn't the one telling, but it does hold the space for you to hear the message. So time is of the essence! Time and change go together in life. You have both to further your purpose. Find your purpose in three easy steps.

Step One: Take a Stance in Who You Are

You're in this body, with this family of sorts, personality, attitudes, thoughts, actions, and reactions. Accept it as it is. It's already doing the best job it can. Notice what you don't like about yourself, how you respond, what you could have done better. Accept that. And make the decision to change. Don't worry about how, when, or why right now. Just decide to change that which you don't like. Keep a book of change around and write one aspect of change a week. The following week, see how change happened and write I Did It, followed by what change you achieved.

Step Two: Decide Where to Be

We are all in relationship with each other and the great news is, we can be with whoever and wherever we want to be. Right now, we are with those who align to us, wanted or not. So focus on who you wish to align more with, and where. If you have time, take a piece of paper and write in detail where and with what type of people you desire to be. If you are looking for an apartment to rent, tour areas you would love to live in. If you wish for more uplifting relationships, read, listen, chat, go to places where you may find those people. If you desire more money, align with people and places where it is in abundance. Your soul's spirit will elevate the minute you connect with spaces and relationships you'd rather be in.

Step Three: Express Your Soulful Self

Only after step one and two will you be able to express yourself from your soul's perspective rather than from the outside personality it has taken on. If you have understood in step one that your personality is your external expression and your spirit your internal expression, then you can match your soul expression to who you think you are, inside and out. Challenge yourself.

Take a selfie (a picture of yourself) and observe yourself. Let your kid take a mini movie of you on your birthday. Go on a radio show; notice how you react to speaking to different people. Who are you when you express yourself? Is this the "you" that you want to be? This is the moment your soul can hear, feel, or see itself through its chosen experience. Make it worth your soul's life story.

Epilogue

Throughout our many lives as souls we learn more about ourselves. I like to point out the fact that it is our great Brilliant Essence we are exploring; the essence of our brilliant selves. The land we walk on, the scents we smell, what we hear, feel, see, experience in and all around us are on our path of discovery. This to me includes the unseen.

What kept me going in my faith and beliefs in times of doubt and ridicule is the fact that communicating with spirit and souls has tremendously helped me in my life. The more I acknowledged an answer, the better I lived and the better I became. The better I became, the prouder I was of myself. I became happier, more fulfilled than ever before. Souls in the afterlife have a huge part in my life, as they do for everyone, even if they remain unseen. From life through death and into the afterlife, souls continue to engage and disengage with each other in more ways than one. Connection and communication never cease. It is time to acknowledge the reality of our kinship and share in better ways our journeys.

After reading the book, it may not surprise you to know that this book also has a soul. Spirit consciousness flows in it. It can be a friend. It talks to you. It makes you feel. Words whispered, with a taste of heart and a smell of, well, paper or pad, the book is alive to serve. As I worried about the content of the book, someone on the other side reminded me that it was already gifted with humor, wisdom and smarts, and that it was like "my baby". Emotions of intense love and, well, motherhood flowed through me as I held up the book in my mind with praise. This book will change lives, I thought, because it is filled with hope; the same hope souls in the afterlife have told me was what drew them to reincarnate.

I wish to leave you with one last message from us all here connected within Brilliant Essence in regards to the question, What's next? When you consider that being and connecting is relative to a state of consciousness, then it is easy for you to understand that there are many other forms and worlds of being, each with their relative states of consciousness, and that it is therefore very simple to communicate with each and all should you simply dial the frequency of your own state of consciousness to match those of others. Happy travels!

About the Author

Astrid Stromberg is celebrated as a gifted international inspirational and motivational speaker.

Born a psychic medium, her advice is sought by the famous plus people from all walks of life to channel messages from beyond for their personal and professional success. She has travelled the world learning from many faiths and practices.

She is a certified mediator, former president to the United Nations Association for Northern California, radio and TV producer and host. Past experience in business development keys her into the economy. Her gifts include: holistic healer, certified clinical hypnotherapist, Reiki master, ordained minister, teacher, artist, and astrologer. In her spare time she assumes her role as a homeschooler. (it's really visa versa!)

Astrid loves tennis, horseback riding, travel and cultural pursuits. She is the mother of two and founder of Brilliant Essence. Astrid resides in the mountains of California where she enjoys the spirits of nature and communes with its riches among her family and friends.

www.BrilliantEssence.com

Quips from Astrid

- Personal motto: everything and anything is possible!
- Flip off negatives and instill a positive in yourself.
- Allow yourself to be. Just be more observant of yourself and always reach for better.
- When you want your mind to be proactive, creative, and productive, meditate first.
- Life ain't always easy, but God never gives us more than we can handle. Ever!

Testimonials

"Expect a Miracle when you read Astrid Stromberg's insightful book. Stromberg's credentials, including her status as a Certified Clinical Hypnotherapist, spring to life with exciting revelations on Dying and Living. Her sensitive probes to after-life are gifts for the soul and answer so many of the perplexing questions all of us have considered. No more fears or tears after you read "What's Next?" A treasure of a book from one of the most heralded heaven-sent authors you will ever read!" ~Leona M. Merrin, author of "Standing Ovations: Devi Dja, Woman of Java"

"The greatest mystery of human existence is what happens to us, and our loved ones, when we die. Both sages and scientists have attempted to tackle this difficult subject, one that often brings up great fear and anxiety. Astrid Stromberg offers a powerful and inspiring guide to her own vast research and personal insight into death and rebirth, and what happens to our souls in during and in between. This book is both educational and enlightening and covers everything from the soul's purpose to how we choose our families and loved ones before we are born, to predestined events and blueprints for soul growth, and the long journey our souls take both in the classroom of life and the classroom of death. This amazing book delivers not just tons of information, but experiences and exercises that will help the reader understand the process of death, and rebirth, in a way that removes fear and instead brings out the "brilliant essence" of who we really are, where we came from, and where we are going." ~Marie D. Jones, best selling author of Destiny Vs. Choice: The Scientific & Spiritual Evidence Behind Fate and Free Will.

"This book is Brilliant!" ~Bruce Merrin, CEO, Celebrity Speakers Entertainment.

Printed in the United States
By Bookmasters